HEALING TRAUMATIZED CHURCHES

A Journey Towards Healthy, Faithful Resiliency in Drama Format

by
Pastor Ronald H. Wean, MDiv, MEd, LPCC,
HTC MINISTRIES, LLC

www.priorspress.com

IN MEMORIAM
Kay Frances Wean
Brave, beloved artist and co-author, SGD

and

DEDICATED TO

Dr. Sabiers and the courageous team at the
bone-marrow transplant unit
of
Miami Valley Hospital, Dayton, Ohio

CONTENTS

FOREWORD

A Quote from Healing Traumatized Churches:
"There are no classes taught in seminary to
understand the dynamics of trauma—how it
affects individuals and how traumatizing leadership impacts organizations. Based on a first
responder study, spirituality is the best predictor of post-trauma growth, yet not a single book
talks about the theology of trauma, it's healing
and teaching." (Chapter 5)

In my morning meditation, I came across this prayer: "Lord, guide
us to act, live, and pray as the times determine. Make our faith grow
to accommodate the needs of your people and the fulfilment of your
kingdom."[1] As I utter the prayer, my attention was caught by the
phrase "to act, live, and pray as the times determine." This book is
written in and for these times in the life of the church.

You are holding in your hands a timely contribution toward
mending the fabric of relationships in the community of faith. Who
is not aware of a church that has been shocked or deeply troubled
by internal and external behaviors, decisions, or experiences? More
likely, most of us have been or are a part of such a church.

---

[1] Claiborne, Wilson-Hartgrove, and Ikoro, *Common Prayer: A Liturgy for
Ordinary Radicals* (Zondervan, 2010) p. 174 Check source book for proper way
to cite. You normally include first names, as well as place of publication.]

In recent decades, we have finally mustered the courage to react to the coercive and abusive leadership behaviors in the church and to ultimately identify and respond to its effects. While there is a crack in this great wall of silence, churches and their leaders are still ill-equipped to address and integrate the experience of trauma after it has occurred. Any kind of trauma is a challenge, there is no question about that. What makes it more difficult is our relationship with the person or group of people that cause us such trauma. It tears at the social fabric—the intricate web of relationships that makes the church a community of faith and witnesses together.

The first thing you will notice about this book is its unusual presentation: the dramatic format. Since the ancient Greeks' time, a dramatic presentation has been used to convey compelling messages from the speakers and writers to their target listeners. And its effectiveness never failed. By merely watching actors from the balcony, by carefully observing the lives portrayed on the stage, we instantly "get it." We laugh and cry, sharing every emotion with the characters. We accept or despise their flaws. Similarly, we offer redemption and forgiveness, too. In witnessing the lives that they portray, we discover unrealized hope for our own.

This book aims to achieve the same impacts that Greek dramas have imparted on us. With this book's dramatic format, we can touch a complicated and often out-of-reach subject. We are invited into a healing room, yet we are not forced into it. We are inspired to see things differently, to realize the "unusual in the usual things." As a result, we are invigorated to bring light and healing to dark corners and spaces that have eluded us. At multiple levels, we are inspired to develop a renewed understanding about ourselves and about the lives that we share with one another in our faith communities. We are taken out of isolation and invited into communion.

Ron draws upon his extensive professional experience of walking persons through post-trauma reaction and introduce them into new lives of wholeness and post-trauma growth. He effectively used language and conversation to bring his knowledge of trauma theory to practice. Through language, we can name and share our experiences. Through dialogue, we learn the importance of social engagement in our healing. Like a hand to a glove, trauma language and conversation perfectly goes with one another. Using a language and sharing our trauma in conversation with one another unites us as human beings and unleashes energy for ministry and mission.

Thus, a theme of hope, resurrection, and renewal runs through this book. Persons in a faith community can discover new mutuality levels—a fresh experience of care and support to and from one another. There are no boundaries. A congregation can break through the stale, stagnant, and take-no- risk, controlled existence. It can be free once again, rediscovering the Spirit- given energy and life. This is not entirely for the church's sake; it is also for the sake of the shared gospel mission of all churches.

Jesus said, "You are the light of the world… You are the salt of the earth" (Matt. 5:14, 13). A congregation that has become cranky, controlling, and numb because of ignored post-trauma reaction has lost its saltiness. How can its saltiness be restored? It is the work of the Holy Spirit to transform our lives to be salt and light for the sake of the world God loves—to become a taste of the kingdom.

Ron reminds us that healing from trauma is not by our efforts alone. Transformed trauma is a transformation into the heart of the gospel, and this is the specialized work of the Holy Spirit in the life of the church. The gospel says that God is in our trauma, that in the cross, God has become the Traumatized One for us. Where a faith community learns to claim this promise and seeks to embody it in its life and relationships, it becomes a good news community more and more—the kind that our trauma-stricken world needs and longs to see.

This is not a call for perfection, but rather, a call for the church to become a Christ in the world: a wounded healer. As a faith community, our journey involves being aware of our pains and actively seeking healing. It requires us to become attentive to our failures and to consequently seek forgiveness. It is not despite failures, hurts, and trauma, but *because* of them, the church can make Jesus Christ visible in the world in faithful and credible ways.

This book invites congregations to claim and live out their trust in the Traumatized One—the Crucified and Risen One. For this to happen, new vision and new ways of thinking and behaving will be needed. Church leaders must become equipped with skills, support, and resources to cultivate fruitful conversation and care more honestly for one another. To this end, Ron makes a significant contribution.

This is deep and passionate labor of love. I am grateful for the gifts that are evident here—gifts of the Spirit for the sake of the church's part in God's mission in today's world. Here is nearly a whole lifetime of integrating critical frameworks and practices for healing with a church's love while being steeped in the dramatic arts. This creative work is a gift to the church and to me.

Pastor Dale Ziemer, MDiv, MAASB
The Center for Parish Development
Palatine, Illinois Easter, 2012

Introduction:

Why Write About Church Trauma?

When faced with significant life challenges that are physically, emotionally, mentally, or spiritually damaging, what are your typical response? Do you hide? Do you run? Or do you face the problem head-on? You are the driver of your own life outcome, the same way that your church leaders are the ones that set sail for your church. So, what should the church do in case of trauma?

Over the past thirty-four years, I have witnessed how leadership aggression led to three separate cases of traumatized churches. What these churches thought as small wounds turned out to be their long-term torment. In fact, even after decades, those same churches remained unhealthy—cranky, controlling, and numb. They exhibited little life for evangelism, mission, or stewardship.

What the three churches failed to apply is plain simple yet often overlooked. They were unable to use creative, logical, and emphatic means of healing their trauma. And instead of healing, what they did was to bury the problem. They buried it under the tombstone with a mark saying, "JUST MOVE ON!"

So, when I saw the fourth church conducting the same burial ritual, the same method that the other three churches did, I felt obliged to start this writing. To finally talk about healing trauma and its applications and importance to traumatized churches.

The human body's physiological response to trauma is often unpleasant, so wanting to bury trauma is nothing unnatural. In fact, it is natural and partially understandable. However, the problem with this form of response is that we do not bury the trauma alone. Together with it, faith is also entombed.

Come to think of it. If a church can't be honest and responsible enough to heal its own history, how can it even earn, redeem, and keep its people's trust?

The credibility of the witnesses of God's healing power can be proven based on their response to trauma. A credible witness will intentionally heal trauma, while the untrustworthy will wish to bury it instead. So, a church that hides the truth instead of embracing and responding to it is very likely to be dishonest, unreliable, unhealthy, and unsafe.

Sadly, the congregations who practice burying painful truth begin to look like battle-weary first responders. Looking at them through the lenses of healing trauma, it is apparent how the acts of forgetting and leaving the truths behind look nothing different from the Grinch that stole the church!

Always remember that moving forward without seeking resolutions does not fix trauma, nor does it help the church in any way. It is an ineffective band-aid solution to a painful yet temporary situation that could have been solved through acceptance and implementing a healing plan instead of simply moving on.

When faced with significant life challenges that are damaging physically, emotionally, mentally, or spiritually, what are your typical response? Do you hide? Do you run? Or do you face the problem head-on? A second natural reaction to trauma is to grab for control. This is a survival mechanism that counters the feeling of being helpless throughout the course of the traumatic experience. It is the fight, flight, or freeze response that we often hear when talking about emergencies and uncontrolled situations.

When seeking control, expect to see three types of people—the fighters, fliers, and freezers. Freezers are the people who, when faced with trauma, ball up and play dead in a surrender posture. The fliers fly and run away from the trauma. Finally, the fighters are the people who opt to stay and face the trauma by micro-managing everyone and everything, around them. This same pattern of reactions is also seen in traumatized churches. In a post-trauma church, the fighters do take charge of the trauma, with the goal of finally ending the sufferings. The freezers, on the other hand, are the ones submissive to the demands imposed by the fighters. Of course, there are also fliers. These people respond to the trauma by being physically and emotionally disengaged with the congregation.

And this is where things get tricky. The fighters believe they are helping the congregation by taking charge, centralizing power, and structuring top-down decision-making. However, it has the opposite effect. Grabbing administrative control in a traumatized church has the same effect as treating sick people with bloodletting, it only makes them sicker!

Congregations need to be empowered to embrace and heal their own trauma. Grabbing organizational control through administrative decision making not only blocks the healing of the congregation, but also condemns the church to manifest the three post-traumatic symptoms: being cranky, controlling, and numb.

Church leadership seizing control through "martial law" is like being swept away in a flood, seeing an alligator swim by, and grabbing onto the alligator's back, reasoning, "I'm relieved, because at least the alligator knows where it's going!" Doesn't make sense, does it?

Therefore, using the two short-term strategies of burying trauma and alligator grabbing are deadly poisons to the long-term life and health of traumatized churches. They block trauma survivors from becoming trauma thrivers: the living evidence that God brings new life from trauma.

So why would churches use dead-end, unhealthy strategies instead of just merely healing the trauma? Well, the problem is we have no language to describe church trauma. The language of trauma belongs to the first-responder community, not to the church. Productive healing conversations for churches will not happen without a common, shared language of trauma.

Using meaningless words to address painful eventsonly yields nonsense. Like a traumatized person, a traumatized church does not need the generic advice like, "Give it time," "It will all work out in the end," or "Everything will be all right." Those things would typically be the first thing that would come to mind. But the fact that people or churches continue to be in post-trauma reaction following a traumatic event only means that those pieces of advice are not working. In fact, they have no track record of ever working with anyone or any organization in healing trauma. Truth be told. There is a desperate need to translate languages of trauma to develop logical, creative, and empathetic healing plans and actions. Without a deliberate, structured plan or protocol for healing, churches would remain stuck with trauma, the failed burial of trauma, and control grabbing to keep it buried. So there is no spectrum of choices because there are only two possibilities, either the church is actively healing itself, or it is passively burying the trauma.

When I started recognizing the pivotal role of translation in church healing, I stopped talking and started translating. A translation from counselor/first-responder language to a common language was needed to begin trauma conversations in wounded churches. This book was written to make those healing conversations possible and to allow healing plans to arise.

Healing Traumatized Churches is a translation that provides a language framework to assist trauma-surviving churches in becoming trauma-thriving churches. With knowledge and compassion, churches can identify post-trauma reactions and respond to them creatively, logically, and empathetically through healing activities. Empowered church leadership needs to be a healing servant of congregational trauma instead of an undertaker in its burial. Churches either directly plan for trauma's healing or are simply haunted by it.

Is your church haunted by past, unredeemed trauma? Trauma is patient and will not be ignored. Like the trauma symbolized by the snake Moses lifted up in the wilderness (see Numbers 21), it needs to be lifted up and not be buried. And who has been chosen by God to lift up the traumatized than the church of the Traumatized One, the One whom God lifted up? Who has God called and equipped to assist in trauma's redemption than those who pick up the cross and follow the One who became trauma's Redeemer? Lastly, who better to engage in healing conversations than the people whose God became a trauma *for* them?

Therefore, with a worldwide burgeoning number of traumatized people, the church of the Traumatized One has many ministry opportunities. However, even though the harvest is plentiful, why are the laborers so few? Churches actively engaged in healing instead of burying their trauma will be lifted up, redeemed, and empowered to reach out to the majority of the un-churched traumatized population.

Therefore, this book is dedicated to healing the physiological, relational and spiritual chaos created by church trauma. Post-trauma healing and growth give the church the nets to go fishing. The good news is that the church *has* the "good news": God has decided to save us through the trauma of the cross. Through the Traumatized One, God, resurrects, uplifts, and redeems all trauma. Therefore, as we learn through that holy trauma, the Redeemer continually redeems our trauma, raising it to become our healing teacher so that we may not just survive, but thrive.

This book has three goals: (1) to translate the first-responder language in order to create a language framework for healing, (2) to use that a framework to establish church organizational structures supportive of healing conversations, (3) to invoke reflections and thinking through the questions, and (4) to present trauma theory and theology in an educational drama format. An expansion of the three goals is found in the appendix.

The inspiration for *Healing Traumatized Churches* came from my wife, Kay Frances. Her talent to "look at the usual unusually" propelled both her creativity and her empathy. Her inspiration led me to use post-trauma assessments "unusually" in order to view traumatized churches. God's goodness continues to shine through her— my brave, beloved artist, and co-author.

Discussion Questions

1. We've already established that exposure to leadership aggression can traumatize churches. We've also learned that wanting to bury these events and simply hoping to move forwards is a natural reaction to the trauma. But like every existing physiological and mental trauma among humans, would that mean that there is a trigger that makes this resurface? If so, what are they?

2. "Trauma is patient and will not be ignored," quite a far-fetched discussion to provoke. But is it possible that acknowledgment and conversation on the topic is an insufficient response, and churches can only be healed through creative actions?

3. How will the people and the churches be affected by healing trauma? How exactly significant is the process of healing traumatized church to people?

Possible Responses to DQ

1. We can deduct from reading the introduction that the triggers of church trauma are deeply buried traumatic experiences and nonsense phrases such as "Give it time" or "Everything will be alright." These statements tend to invalidate and push the trauma deeper, which can cause it to burst, similar to bottled up emotions.

2. Achieving collective action is difficult to attain, but it is possible. If left untouched, even if not totally buried, trauma can grow until it reaches a point of no turning back. Talking about the traumatic experience can somehow alleviate the building up of emotions, but the long-term solution can only be attained through empathetic, logical, and creative actions.

3. As stated in the text, "Post-trauma healing and growth give the church the nets to go fishing." A church free from post-

trauma reactions has people free from the confines of phys-iological, traumatic emotions and encounters, which tend to poison the essence of the church itself. We must take action regarding this topic. Even if it is only acknowledging and initiating the discussion, it is one big step in making quite the difference.

CHAPTER 1:

The Dead Rat in the Wall

Have you ever been caught in a situation that you yourself do not understand? What would you do if you found yourself in the middle of a vicious cycle that doesn't seem to have a start and an end? Do you play the fool and act as nothing is happening? Do you try to solve the problem on your own? Or do you just leave everything behind and move sideways instead of forward?

Commentary

Trauma happens. It happens suddenly, and no individual nor group is invulnerable. It surprises us, overwhelms our coping skills, and leaves us feeling the terror of powerlessness. It makes us lose control over our lives. Even a simple prank can be traumatizing, or trigger a post trauma reaction.

People who survive trauma's actual or perceived lethal threat are changed forever. Some survivors become thrivers. They grow from the experience and develop a deeper understanding of themselves and their connection with God and with other people. This pattern of surviving and thriving is what we call *post-trauma growth*.

However, many churches fail to achieve this growth. They stagnate even at the earliest stages of survival; thus, they never experience thriving and growing out of their trauma.

The bigger problem is that, because these churches failed to survive, they search for another escape, which they often find through burying their trauma. Instead of learning from the event, they bury and belittle their traumatic experience, pretending that it didn't happen at all. As a result, their post-traumatic identities become disconnected, controlling, cranky. They become numb to their feelings and to the feelings of others.

I know one traumatized church that was not satisfied with merely surviving. It took its trauma one step ahead and engaged itself to a healing plan that helped them thrive. After going through the healing process, the church now experiences a deeper understanding and connection with God and others. They are now thrivers whose trauma has been transformed and lifted up to become their life teacher.

The Five Steps of Healing

You might be wondering how did the church heal itself from trauma. Here is a walk through the courageous yet straightforward five-step healing plan that they took.

The first step is simple. To start its healing, the church made a courageous choice of healing its trauma rather than burying it. The church did not hide nor conceal the fact that they had been traumatized by a savage leadership. It accepted the reality that it was a herd of sheep that have been fleeced by the shepherd!At church, we lay our trust upon the leaders. We often look up to our leaders as shepherds who are supposed to understand their roles—"The good shepherd lays down his life for the sheep." However, what happens to traumatized churches is something different. Instead of protecting the sheep, the shepherd betrayed and cooked them! And once that happens, churches can only begin a healing journey by embracing the pain of betrayal and accept the reality that they had been burned!

The second step towards healing was surrendering what the church thought reality should be. The church that I've known forgot about their "good shepherd and church expectations" such as:

"My pastor, called by God, should never hurt me."

"All pastors should be good shepherds."

"Nothing wrong should ever happen here because we are a good church, and God always blesses good churches."

"Only nice people attend here."

Instead of hanging on to these false expectations, the church courageously decided to stop living in denial and face their reality. They let go of their "should be's" and accepted their "what are's."

This part of their healing journey was painfully brought home to me by a New York City mugging of a family member. Not that muggings are all that unusual in big cities, but this mugging occurred in the middle of Time Square at five-thirty in the afternoon. The family relative was surrounded by twenty thousand people and two hundred police officers but was assaulted by two adolescent females. When asked, "What happened?" the relative replied, "I was with all these people...I thought I should be safe, so I let my guard down. And I learned that I will never do that again."

Learning from painful experiences of life is called wisdom. And persistent holding on to the "should be's" of painful experiences is called plain foolishness. Despite this truth being as clear as the sun, many churches, like many people, still choose to pursue folly, dig in their heels, and learn nothing from life's painful lessons.

The third courageous decision the church made was to talk honestly to each other about their ordeal. They decided to break the pattern of dishonesty, deception, and blame. They agreed on "the truth, the whole truth, and nothing but the truth" from each other. They took a leap of faith in God and believed the promise that "the truth shall set you free."

The fourth courageous decision was to ask for help. The church did not have any language or framework to communicate—let alone process what had happened. The good news is that they asked for help from a bishop who took their pain seriously; a "good shepherd" who creatively, logically, and empathetically cared for the sheep. This bishop did not react with anxiety in order to save the institution, but instead responded with the right plan for healing.

Unfortunately, not all churches are lucky enough to meet a bishop with the same mindset towards trauma. In fact, most church leaders at almost all levels tend to react negatively when asked for help regarding church trauma. They tend to respond with anxiety and resort to the classic advise of moving on by burying it.

But this particular bishop went against the grain. With wisdom, the bishop gave them the resources. He supplemented them not just with the right words but also with a language framework that helped them process and learn from their trauma. The bishop showed the path by encouraging them to do a congregational book study using the book *People of the Lie* by Dr. Scott Peck.

Finally, the fifth courageous action and decision were to heal. Everyone in the congregation made a commitment to have conversations using the bishop's recommended reading. Armed with a language framework from the book, they were able to process and make sense of what had happened to them. After several months, they felt empowered with wisdom. They felt free to share their experiences, strength, and hope with one another. They rejoiced together that God had brought them through the valley of the shadows.

Now, they remember the past with understanding and gratitude for both the healing presence of God and each other. They have renewed energy to spread the good news of God's healing goodness. The church's leadership did not rely on reactionary organizational development schemes or top down administrative decision making to bury both their anxiety and trauma. Instead, they developed their own five-step plan of healing, and on top of that, they created a plan of action to address any future trauma.

Typical Responses to Trauma

Without a deliberate healing plan to directly address the trauma, the stakes become very high. For example, the lack of a healing plan can make the traumatized may become another traumatizer. The traumatized are very likely to apply the Golden Rule in reverse, to *do things unto others before others get an opportunity to do it back to them.* This fight response prompts the church to mimic the traumatizer in order to protect itself from the imminent danger.

Other churches may have a more passive reaction to trauma. This surrender-and-freeze response turns the Golden Rule sideways, *don't do anything so that no one will do anything to you.* While it may put your unpleasant experience to a halt, the freeze reaction still invites a continuation of trauma.

Furthermore, others will hit the bricks and flee to another church in the aftermath of trauma. To them, the Golden Rule is to leave before others have a chance to do it to them again. These folks are usually called names like "church hoppers." They either hop out of the fear of being traumatized again or avoid any situations that bring even a hint of anxiety. They either react by saying, "I come to church just to worship; I don't want to get involved," or react the way many unchurched people do, saying, "Hell will freeze over before I ever go to any church ever again!"

Churches without structured healing plans are left with the blended children of trauma—a mixture of traumatizers and surrenderers. Many of those who flee are already gone or at least have no desire to get involved. Thus, the foxes (fighters) and the chickens (freezers) are left to share the same home! And guess who rises to the top of leadership in those churches?

Under these living arrangements, the mission, and work of the the church is severely compromised. Instead of being "little Christs" to one another, churches continue the cycle of being traumatizing to one another. The surrenderers are left with no chance and choice; they continue to play dead and let the fighters run everything and run over everyone.

The church, therefore, becomes unsafe and unhealthy. Instead of taking responsibility for their own feelings and actions and sharing their experiences, strengths, and hope, the church starts to stink with hidden agendas, ideology, and blaming power struggles.

Anyone who happens to wander into a church that is struggling in post trauma survival can smell the decaying dead rat inside the wall, despite the church looking all beautiful on the outside.

When churches are traumatized, the terror of trauma is intense because the stakes are high. Eternal life—not just this life—is threatened because "if this is how God is represented, I want no part of God!" This intense reaction may be one reason why the dead rat can stay in the wall for centuries.

The following story describes a traumatized church that is stuck in its post-trauma stage for four hundred years! Trauma's footprints continued to walk in the church for generations. The church is already disconnected from the long-forgotten original trauma, yet ironically, is still held by the same controlling organizational structure used by the original traumatizer.

A Church Parable

There once was a Protestant church that was several hundred years old. It was a typical European church except for one odd ritual. Whenever church members entered the sanctuary, before sitting in their pews, they turned to a blank wall and bowed.

However, when visitors asked, "Why do you bow to a blank wall?" the church members replied, "We don't know. This is what we are supposed to do. It's always been done."

Whenever new people join the church and press for answers on "*why they need to bow to a blank wall,*" the established members become defensive and retort with the generic statements,

> "Look, our parents and our parents' parents all bowed to the blank wall. We were taught in catechism, 'When entering the church, bow to that wall.' So, all members in good standing will continue to bow to that wall. Those who cannot bow don't belong. Any more questions?"

Thus, the members continued to bow to the blank wall without an understanding of the origin of the peculiar behavior. When questioned, they simply resorted to defending the action rather than becoming curious and asking the same question that all outsiders have asked: "Why do we bow to this blank wall?"

As time passed, the church saw the need for repair and renovation. It just so happened that the work to be done required digging into that very same blank wall!

When the renovation began, the workers peeled off several layers of plaster and discovered a beautiful icon of Mother Mary. For some reason, she had been covered up for four hundred years since the Reformation, and no one knew that she was behind the blank wall.

Faced with this mysterious treasure, the church finally became curious about who they were and how they came to be. They began to search for an explanation as to how Mary had remained hidden behind plaster for four hundred years, and possibly even solve the second mystery of *how did we come to bow to this blank wall?*

In searching for the truth of this mystery, the church decided that they wanted to know their own history. They made a commitment to have a conversation to discover their identity, uncover the the mystery of Mary, and unlock the secrets of their own odd behavior.

In their search for truth, they were surprised to discover that before the Reformation, the church had been Roman Catholic. After the Reformation, the land was ruled by a Protestant prince. This prince forced Protestant doctrine on Catholics, offending their consciences. He traumatized the Catholic membership and forced them to abandon their expression of faith.

To ensure that the church would remain Protestant, the prince further used his centralized power and top-down medieval-management decision-making to desecrate the church. He either removed or covered up any reminders of the Roman Catholic faith. Mary's picture could not be removed, so it was covered up with four inches of plaster. The prince then forbade them to talk about the event, telling them, "This is God's will."

However, even with the Catholic faith's last remnant removed and Mary's icon covered, the people remained Roman Catholic. With their last ounce of courage and conviction, they hung on to their identity as Roman Catholics.

In self-defining but dangerous defiance, the people continued to bow to Mary's blank wall. Even with Mary covered, the faithful reacted as Roman Catholics through the continued bowing. It was a sign of identity and strength in the face of tyranny. Without question, they knew who they were: Roman Catholic Christians.

However, these people were not allowed to talk about their traumatic experience. Faced with a capital crime if they talked, they never processed their anguish over their defiled consciences from the abuse of centralized power and unilateral decision- making. Consequently, because they were forbidden to speak, no learning ever occurred. Instead, it was buried in the backyard of the church's collective consciousness, and soon enough was forgotten. Only this odd, post-trauma, blank-wall-bowing remained as a clue that something traumatizing had ever happened.

So initially, this odd ritual of bowing to a blank wall was really an act of self-definition in the face of tyranny, a fight for identity and control of one's own conscience. Without the ability to speak and process the trauma, their own history became a mystery. The people could never embrace their strength, lift up their identity, or celebrate their power in defying the tyranny of forced conversions. Bowing to a blank wall was their only way to show their powerful oppressor that despite doing his worst, the people remained faithful Roman Catholics. In bowing, they found some measure of control in their loss of control.

However, when the church's trauma history became disconnected to the post-trauma reaction of bowing, there could be no celebration of the community's power, strength, or identity. They were left with a four-hundred-year-old odd ritual, an inexplicable but well-defended abnormal reaction—much to the world's scorn and derision.

Now how could this abnormal reaction have been passed down from generation to generation? Each generation had to be taught, told, and scolded to "Bow to the wall! No questions! It's God's will!" In other words, how could a silly ritual be continued unless it was forced?

Paradoxically, did the leadership in each generation use the same methods as the Protestant prince—abuse of power, forced conversions, and violations of conscience? Therefore, instead of the church being a safe and healthy instrument of healing, was each new generation traumatized into bowing to a blank wall as well?

For generations, the faithful unknowingly continued to react in the same way they had reacted when they were first traumatized. Without knowing their true identity, they could not embrace or gain strength from it. Instead, their identity became linked to this odd post-trauma reaction. Their motivation became "God wants you to bow to blank walls."

Does the Traumatized One call the church just to witness these scenes? Or is the church called for a greater good—to be a safe place for the traumatized, a healing place, and a hospitable place to engage in trauma conversations?

Yet, how did this odd post-trauma reaction continue for four hundred years? Simply put, it became part of the organizational foundation and structure.

They had no trauma conversations because they were forbidden to have a language for it. Without those conversations, the following generations did not know their own history, identity, or truth. And since their own story was blocked, these survivors unknowingly organized their community in reaction to the traumatic experience by seizing control and abusing power, just like what the Protestant prince had done. In biting irony, in their pursuit to show their faithfulness, they had become the same image of the prince.

How could they not use their educational system to make sure the blank-wall-bowing continued? How could the leadership not socialize the new members: "Bow to the blank wall, or be different from the rest of us?"

The Protestant prince, therefore, thoroughly succeeded. By forbidding the people to speak, they buried the trauma and forgot who they were. He successfully programmed their reactions for the next four hundred years. Each new generation of leaders socialized the congregation to follow the original gag order: "Don't talk or question; bow to the blank wall!"

Those survivors of the trauma organized themselves based on the traumatic experience. They continued the post-trauma reaction through the same medieval-management style modeled by the Protestant prince: a centralized power with top-down, unilateral decision-making. Through the organizational structure, these post-trauma reactions continued long after the original trauma had disappeared.

In this parable, we can see the importance of an intentional healing plan. Without it, the traumatized get stuck bowing to walls, an odd, senseless, life-limiting, and attention-grabbing activity. They impeded the church's mission and made the church unsafe, unhealthy, and an horrendous witness.

How many congregations do you know that are still being held by the blank wall?

Reader's Theatre

Act 1, Scene 1: The Post-Meeting Parking Lot

The setting is a church parking lot following a church meeting. John, a church council member, joined pastors Mark and Lucy. Mark has served as senior pastor for nine years, while Lucy has served eight years.

All three have just attended an informational congregational meeting that once again ended with sudden shouting, threats, and silence.

As John walks toward his car, he is joined by his two pastors, Mark and Lucy. Both are wearing clergy attire.

JOHN: I'm glad you both are here. I gotta talk before going home.
     That meeting. It-it really made me mad.
LUCY: We have more where that came from! Going back for seconds?

MARK: Or to the bar to spend money you don't have with people who don't care?

JOHN: I know. We've been here before—after church meetings, standing here in the parking lot…with you two helping me not to go home "cranky," as my youngest calls me.

LUCY: Is it the "sudden shouter," the "resentfully silent" or the ones threatening to leave the church that gets you?

MARK (*interrupting*): None of the above. It's boredom.

JOHN: Boredom? How can you be bored when the church is stuck—stuck in bad reruns? It's almost like a hostage situation! But a hostage to what? I don't even know. It just feels like I'm a hostage.

MARK: Well, I'm not going to be a hostage to boredom. It's the same old movie over and over—just a different day, a different meeting, and it's *bor-or-ing*!

JOHN: What a mystery that we can't end the meetings *before* the ritual yelling and threats to leave the church starts!

MARK: And it's so automatic! I attend Rotary and Toastmasters with these same people, and they never do it there. And yet, here in church, it's 'there she blows!'

LUCY: Agreed. It's unnerving, just waiting for the blowups—blowups with no causes and no explanations.

JOHN (*pausing*): We're just not seeing the obvious.

MARK AND LUCY: Seeing the what?

JOHN: Seeing the obvious. My chemistry professor defined a genius as someone who sees the obvious.

MARK: Yes! We aren't seeing the obvious. (*Long pause*) But what's so obvious?

LUCY (*in a voice imitating the Emerald City guard*): "It's as plain as the nose on my face!"

MARK (*realization dawning*): John, *you* are a genius! There is a piece missing. It's a huge piece, and it's right under our noses!

JOHN: (*pausing, then carefully choosing his words*): I don't even know why I'm bringing this up now. It's been a long time, years, … and we were told not to talk about this.

"Don't bring it up," they told us. "God wants you to move on. Just pray about it. Forgive and forget," we were told.

But the trouble happened a few years before you two arrived. And it was huge. A previous pastor used people to get whatever he wanted. He didn't care what anyone thought 'cause he was always right. He targeted those who disagreed with him.

As a result, many left the church, particularly the educated women. This particular pastor used doctrine and the Bible to hurt and divide us. He was no shepherd, he was a sheep butcher! He left over a dozen years ago, and quite frankly, I...I don't even remember his name now.

MARK AND LUCY (*in unison*): That's dangerous!

JOHN (*long pause, confusion*): Why? What's dangerous?

MARK (*jokingly*): It's dangerous to tell a narcissist you don't remember their name!

LUCY (*intoned voice full of fake importance*): get...just how important...I am! (*Lucy and Mark laugh.*)

JOHN (*observing as both pastors chuckle*): You both seem to get along well. Your humor makes you a good team, an excellent fit.

MARK (*still joking*): It's that *obvious,* huh?

LUCY: Without humor, I couldn't do these meetings. We just don't take ourselves too seriously anymore.

MARK: Not us! Because it's not about us—it's all about God. But narcissists...they're different. They think it's all about them, so they don't share with others or play nice in the sandbox. When it's all about me, I'll do or say whatever to charm others just to get what I want.

LUCY (*laughing*): We know who we are, and we are *not* the ones in charge. We're in sales, not the general manager of the universe. But narcissists want total control because they believe they are the universe's GM. But we know who is in charge, don't we, Mark?

MARK: Sure do. And it ain't us! But I must confess, I have a fantasy— to have five minutes, just five minutes to be the Almighty and stop these bizarre reactions to benign conversations.

LUCY (*sarcastically*): Unfortunately, Mark Almighty, it's still illegal to do brain transplants!(*She becomes thoughtful and shifts the topic.*) But something must get these verbal food fights going.

JOHN: Can't get my mind around it, either. I've chaired meetings where no one showed up! (*He is thoughtful.*) They probably wanted to avoid all the sudden drama. (*He pauses.*)

Now I can handle rejection. But the anger outbursts and shout-downs—they just drive me crazy! Oh, did you see how some people tried to flee the scene but couldn't? Their spouses had death grips on their knees.

LUCY (*jokingly*): I'm more partial to the ones who are silent, who just sit there frozen in their seats…like…

JOHN: Like deer in headlights.

LUCY: Yep!

MARK: So we have three kinds of church members: the fighters, the fliers, and the—

LUCY: Don't say it! Just don't say—

MARK: The freezers!

LUCY AND JOHN: Boo-oo-oo! Hiss-s-s! Hang 'em high!

MARK: And yet all three groups do the same thing.

LUCY: Oh, really? They actually have something in common?

MARK (*still joking*): Of course. The one thing that unites them all is this.

JOHN (*After they stop laughing, he continues*): However, considering the negative impact of not listening, that is no joke. How can it be that God hears *our* words, but we don't listen to each other's?

(*Mark and Lucy look at each other and laugh.*)

JOHN (*bewildered*): What's so funny?

MARK: Now that…is obvious!

LUCY: So, when did you decide to come out of the closet?

JOHN: Closet? What closet?

LUCY: You, obviously, are a closet pastor, John!

MARK: You certainly connect the dots. When no one listens, we have no witness to the God who hears.

JOHN (*protesting*): But I know that God listens and is gracious to us. Conversation with God changes everything. It redeems all conversations.

MARK: Good God, he's on a roll!

LUCY: Someone pass the plate. We're having revival!

JOHN: Are you two making fun of me?

MARK AND LUCY: No!

LUCY: But it's for a good cause.

JOHN: What do you mean?

MARK: You're so dead-on. It's scary!

LUCY: We have a witness of God's redemption—patient listening followed by grace. But when we stop listening and start reacting, there is no proof that God even…exists.

JOHN: It's hard to respond with grace when everyone suddenly barks, "Who let the dogs out?"

LUCY: You better be careful, John. That "barking" could get you ordained!

JOHN (*protesting and laughing*): Oh, stop!

LUCY: Stop what? Stop the barking? The avoiding? The blaming? Or the silence? How can we do any mission or stewardship or outreach without any redeeming conversations?

MARK: I've been here awhile, so I've had conversations with everyone in that meeting. I've been in their homes and always have been treated with grace. Their fellowship and intelligent conversations are a joy. But it all disappears when at church.

JOHN: So, you've never noticed the sign on the church doors?

MARK AND LUCY (*simultaneously*): What sign?

JOHN: It's so obvious. It reads, "Park your brains and hearts at the door. Enter at own risk." (*They all laugh.*)

MARK: Hey, you do stand-up! (*He looks at Lucy*) Shall we gather at the river and ordain him *right now*?

LUCY (*singing*): Shall we gather at the river? The beautiful, the beautiful…MARK: All jokes aside, when I come from meetings like this, I wonder what sane person would ever join this happy throng. There's no listening and no grace. It's just not safe nor healthy.

LUCY: I agree. These reactions are disturbing and distancing. And who knows what triggers it? I bet it is just as plain as our own noses!

JOHN: I wonder if the larger church, the church leadership, could help us out with this mess.

LUCY (*She looks at Mark; both burst out laughing*): That settles it. You're ordained!

JOHN: What?

MARK: You know what they say about great minds, don't you? We've already got an appointment with the bishop for next Thursday. You want to come?

LUCY: We can get a quick bite before going. And I do mean quick, don't I, Mark?

MARK: She's the fastest bite in the West. Just inhales the stuff!

LUCY: And we're off to the races! Besides, I get paid with breakfast.

JOHN: You get paid with breakfast? The church pays for your breakfast?

MARK: No, I pay for it.

LUCY (*smiling*): It's payment. He buys me breakfast because he won't go down into the church crawl space.

MARK (*interrupting*): No way! No how!

LUCY: So, whenever he needs something out of the church crawl space…

MARK: It's breakfast with Bonzo! Granola, bananas, and yogurt—and it just disappears.

LUCY: Greased lightning, but without the grease.

MARK: She doesn't do processed foods or grease.

LUCY: Only au naturel.

MARK: And quickly!

LUCY (*looking at John*): So is it breakfast with Bonzo and the bishop?

JOHN: Uh-uh. A little too much…

LUCY: What? You don't think clergy eat?

JOHN: Yes. I mean no! It's just that the two of you, youboth are so honest, transparent. We are so blessed to have you here with us.

LUCY: I feel a group hug coming on.

MARK (*hesitantly*): But before we do that, are you going with us to see the bishop?

JOHN: I'm not going. But I'll do the smart thing.

MARK: Oh yeah? What's that?

JOHN: I'll do breakfast in my kitchen. And *slowly* eat my *processed* food *with* grease…and pray for you both!

MARK: What's that giant clucking sound I hear?

LUCY (*making chicken sounds*): Chick-chick-chick-chickee-ee-ee!

JOHN: Look, you two, my hope goes with you, but my body stays here.

LUCY: Okay, but we'll miss you at the party!

JOHN: Give me a rundown next Sunday. And…be careful.

MARK: Thanks. We'll hang in there.

LUCY: Is it group-hug time?

Discussion Questions

1. The people at the meeting were described as "fighters, fliers, and freezers." Notable, they only react as such at church and not at "the Rotary or Toastmasters." What are the possible explanations to explain the reactions of these folks? What would you call the people who would suddenly react in this manner, seemingly without provocation?

2. "The help you give is only as good as the diagnosis you make." What are the possible negative impacts and consequences to this organization and leadership if the diagnosis turns out to be:
   - they are just screwed up,
   - they have an affinity for chaos,
   - they are a complete mess,

- and quite possibly, they have a personality disorder?

Without a diagnosis, what would leadership attempt to do first?

3. If the congregation leadership attempted to control the aforementioned chaos and mess with organizational savvy and political solutions, would that create a safe and healthy place? Would it create an environment where people can fully experience the healing power, grace, and love God has for all? If you joined a church and discovered that they face anxiety with a fight-flight-freeze norm, what would you do?

4. If you become a leader in a church full of "fighters, fliers, and freezers," what are the first steps you would take to completely and accurately understand and diagnose the situation?

Possible Responses to the DQ

1. Without understanding the issue as a whole, I might base my explanations on their bizarre reactions and conclude that:
   a) these people are *just plain screwed up*
   b) they are *a mess*
   c) they *love chaos*
   d) *they all have a personality disorder*

2. It is highly possible that the group and the leadership will assign a negative connotation to the diagnoses. This may lead to even more *frustration, anger, resentment.*
   Similarly, the diagnosis might create an *adversarial environment* similar to *a labor relations meeting*. The leadership might attempt to assert control of the situation. As such, leadership is likely to:

a) exert grip and put a tight lid on the situation
b) force the rules and doctrines to the members
c) see the discussion as resistance and sabotage
d) pretend that the issues don't exist
e) whitewashing the problems
f) act as if they don't know or they don't care at all

3. It is futile to expect a healthy and stimulating environment from the church unless the original source of the problem is addressed and an appropriate healing plan is developed. If I happen to join a church with the same norm, and I am aware of the power of healing trauma, I will use my voice to raise awareness and develop the appropriate actions.

4. If I become a leader of such a church, my focus would be initiating a deep understanding of the situation. I would ask questions regarding the church's past, present, and future. I would ask about what exactly happened, when did it exactly start, what was the situation, what are their plans for healing. As a new pastor, I would preach and teach the church about healing and take the initiative to plan for the church's recovery.

CHAPTER 2:

When Good Conversations Go Bad

Have you ever been misdiagnosed before? Has someone provided an explanation for your thoughts, experiences, emotions, and sensations without looking at the bigger picture? Have you been told to simply shrug off your fears, anxiety, anger, and other negative thoughts and emotions? In situations like these, were you indecisive of your own feelings and ideas that you accept the misdiagnoses regardless of how insensible they are? Or are you confident and defiant that you insist on what you believe is true and right? How can you tell when the diagnosis is just a guess and not a diagnosis? (Hint: The treatment plan is H.T.T: "Here. Try This!)

Commentary

Do you recognize any fighters, fliers, or freezers in your life? It is likely you do because these three natural reactions are great strategies for surviving the imminent deadly threats of "lions and tigers and bears, Oh my!" However, using these survival strategies in normal problem solving result in lousy discussions and poor decision making. Try talking to people who are at their early post trauma survival stage. Do you expect them to be logical, creative, and empathetic?

More likely, they will either get mad, walk away, or just look at you as if you have three noses!In the meeting, it is evident that something had triggered these natural reactions to danger even though no danger was present. However, the fact that no danger was present did not stop people from reacting with immanent threat survival skills. So, why were the people acting as if the threat was happening right now? And if there was no threat in the present, could the danger have been in the past? And how can you tell if someone is being triggered from past trauma and danger, when the brain cannot tell the difference between memory-triggered traumatic pictures and current threatening events?

For example, one of the greatest films about World War II is *Saving Private Ryan*. When I saw the film, it was in surround-sound on a vast screen. When the troops stormed up Normandy Beach, I saw myself ducking and weaving in my seat, thinking that the bullets were whizzing by my head. At that moment, my brain was not able to distinguish between that flat motion picture on the screen and the real thing. My body reacted as if I was there, trying to survive on that beach.

Three days after watching the movie, I felt like I was still at Normandy. The event kept on running in my mind, and I could not stop the loop that was playing in my mind. Upon reflection, it came to me; How much worse was it for the actual survivors of Normandy? I realized that post-trauma recovery can be measured by whether I could just thoughtfully observe the movie unbothered or react as if I was personally on that bloody beach.

If the trauma from the movie is not processed accordingly, the film will keep on running, and you would always be the star of the show. When triggered, you would feel as if the trauma is happening over and over again in the present. The traumatic images of the past would keep on triggering fight, flight, or freeze responses for survival purposes.

Going back to the church's informational meeting in Chapter 1, it is evident that there are no present stimuli that triggered the commotion. There were no imminent threats, and yet people were reacting as if lions, tigers, and bears were all running loose. How come? Are they just plain nuts? Is that their personality? Or have their trauma memories been triggered, creating a loop of present unhealthy reactions to the past traumatic events?

It does not take much to trigger buried trauma memories and rerun the movie in the present. Fight, flight, or freeze survival reactions can be triggered by a voice, tone, situation, or even a single movement. It is so unpredictable; thus, the need for a deep understanding. Good detective work is needed to find the cause, beginning with Detective Columbo's famous question, "Help Me Understand!"

So, Pastors Mark and Lucy were frustrated because nothing can be accomplished when people suddenly lose their minds and park their brains and hearts at the door. Similarly, the church chaos triggers John's fight reaction is so strong that he carries it with him even after reaching home, as his child often observes.

But if there are no current threats to explain their bizarre reactions, the answer probably lies in the past, right? Did the church experience a danger before? Are their unusual and unhealthy reactions being triggered? Is John stuck in an old movie rerun without him knowing?

Ironically, John remembers the church's trauma event twelve years ago. He has a clear recollection of how the church leadership abused their power to create a division in the congregation. However, John does not realize the connection between his current intense reactions to church meetings and the trauma twelve years ago. That is because back then, he was instructed to simply move-on; thus, he was not able to process the events and trauma accordingly.

As a result, his family has to constantly deal with his "crankiness." In your view, do you see any connection between him being cranky after church meetings and the event that transpired twelve years ago?

So, when people react as if there is a threat when, in fact, there isn't any, the best thing to do is to look at the past. Look for memories that are deliberately buried. There is nothing to lose when you consider the possibility that their reactions are post-traumatic.

Why not do a trauma history and ask, "When did these reactions start?" and "What was going on at the time?" It does not take Sherlock Holmes to find answers because they hide in obvious places.

Not asking questions about the trauma history and not taking them into account is a disservice to the congregation. False diagnoses may take them to defamatory conclusions. In fact, the most common erroneous conclusion for both individuals and churches often relates to their personality.

"That's just the congregation's personality, so there is no changing them."

"That's just the way they are; love them or leave them."

"Those are the weird people who bow to blank walls."

"Those are the people who love to fight [who undermine, are passive-aggressive, who kill their pastors, who are too conservative, who are too liberal, etc.]."

To use a conclusion without investigation is not only irresponsible, but it is also plain wrong. Who wants to get saddled with a personality disorder when the real problem is post-trauma reaction? However, without a language of trauma to provide a meaningful framework, these questions are not asked, and the investigation never happens. As a result, the trauma is buried by the supposed experts themselves.

The Bible gives the best description of the state of the healing arts. The woman with the unstoppable blood flow was described in this manner: "She suffereth much at the hands of physicians." Churches also "suffereth much" at the hands of so-called experts, especially when those experts do not raise trauma questions or do trauma histories.

Twelve years ago, John's church was mistreated, and the mistreatment was delivered by the church expert themselves. John described the mistreatment when the expert told the congregation,

"God wants you to move on."

"Forgive and forget."

"Just pray about it."

The expert used religious-sounding language and gave them a treatment plan to healing without directly dealing with the trauma.

Therefore, in the absence of language, knowledge, and investigation, the treatment was, at best, a guess resulting in buried trauma.

And so the congregation followed a "Here Try This mistreatment plan brought by the unacceptable guessing. People shamed and guilted themselves because they could not follow the plan and have natural reactions to an abnormal situation. They censored themselves. They withheld information about their woundedness—a woundedness that got a backyard religious burial instead of Christ-centered healing.

However, no matter how much burying they do, the trauma resurfaces, whenever triggered, often manifesting itself during church meetings. Thus, we can conclude that though incomplete and the dots are not yet connected, John's beginning assessment was accurate - that the church is stuck and held hostage not by their present circumstances but by their past, unprocessed trauma.

Mark was also right. There is a piece missing, and that missing piece is the inability to recognize the obvious, articulate it, and get a meaningful direction toward healing it. That obvious piece is the *trauma piece*.

Reader's Theatre

Act 1: Scene 2: The Bishop's Office

(*Mark and Lucy are ushered into the bishop's office and sit. Note: The bishop can be either male or female. In this story, the Bishop is male.*)

MARK: We appreciate you taking the time to see us, Bishop.

LUCY: It will be good to get your perspective.

BISHOP: Glad to help any way I can. Now, from your personal summaries and the congregational surveys you both submitted, nothing seems to identify trouble between the two of you. Is there...any that I am unaware of?

LUCY AND MARK (*looking at each other and then to the bishop*): Of course not!

MARK: Why do you ask?

BISHOP: Well, I'm usually the last to know when multi-staff marriages turn sour. And you two have been at this church for well...almost a decade?

MARK: Yes...

BISHOP: And in all that time, there must have been something that has cropped up between the two of you.

LUCY (*pausing, thoughtful*): Well, sometimes he doesn't laugh at my jokes...

MARK: But neither do your kids, so I'm in good company!

BISHOP: Aha! Humor! But does it ever get out of hand? Does it cause resentments or anxiety that the congregation picks up?

MARK (*attempting to refocus the discussion*): Bishop, I appreciate the checkup on our working relationship, but the summaries and surveys detail the the congregation's very odd reactions. They come on suddenly, out of the woodwork and for no apparent reason.

LUCY: And everything comes to a grinding halt: evangelism, mission, stewardship—you name it. And we have searched ourselves and each other, but there are no staff problems. We are blessed with cheerful staff.

MARK: Yes. Believe me, it would be far more comfortable if *we* were the triggering mechanisms of all this...this reactivity...these mountains of molehills.

LUCY: That would be a quick fix to this mystery, but no such luck. So that's why we are here today asking for your help.

BISHOP: I sense your frustration at not finding the answers you seek.

LUCY: Frustrated? Well, perhaps, but it's with my own inability to see the obvious.

BISHOP: What do you mean, "see the obvious"?

LUCY: That's John's phrase, a very active member who defined a genius as one who sees the obvious.

MARK: Which we do not see. And that is why we are here, to see if you can see what we can't see.

BISHOP: So then, let me ask an obvious question: do you think your frustration may be compromising your ability to speak the good news?

LUCY AND MARK: Oh no, absolutely not!

LUCY: God is gracious, loving, and forgiving toward us...

MARK: So that we can be gracious, loving, and forgiving to others.

LUCY: We have no problem preaching of the God who hears us and respond with goodness.

MARK: The problem is, something prevents the congregation from hearing and responding with goodness to each other.

BISHOP: Well, if you two aren't on the verge of a staff divorce, and you both speak and live the good news, then the problem is under some other rock.

LUCY: Under some rock? Why under a rock?

BISHOP: It's an old expression. As kids, we'd go crawdad hunting and look under every rock in the river just in case one was hiding—

LUCY (*interrupting*): I'm from Phoenix. (*Long pause*)

BISHOP (*pausing as well*): Oh! Well, there aren't many rivers out there, are there?

LUCY: No crawdads, either.

MARK (*speaking awkwardly*): So, Bishop, you are looking at all the angles to rule out possibilities. That's understandable. So, what's the next rock to look under?

BISHOP: In reading your continuing-education file, neither of you have attended our church-managers tool shop. It's the latest in management theory. It's quite good, and you might get a lot out of—

MARK (*interrupting*): There is nothing wrong with our organizational leadership, structure, or the way we put together a budget.

LUCY: We hold ourselves and others accountable to the job descriptions.

MARK: And our organizational flow chart is yearly updated. What we are describing is not an organizational issue.

LUCY: So, we don't need to invent another wheel. We need another direction.

MARK: Changing walls and adding bay windows and skylights will not help us fix this problem. It's in the foundation. We have foundational problems— problems that will not change regardless of how many organizational structure changes or management styles we employ.

BISHOP (*getting annoyed*): Well then, have you both tried to modify your approach to the church?

MARK AND LUCY: Our approach?

BISHOP (*catching himself getting annoyed and thus backs it down*): Yes, the ways you approach the flock may be triggering these… these mystery reactions. And if your summaries are accurate, you must be dealing with the personality of the church— their personality quirks. So, you need to learn how to work with them more effectively.

MARK AND LUCY: What?

BISHOP: You have to anticipate their actions. Know your people so you can anticipate their every move. And pay attention to those quirks so you can outmaneuver them, finesse them. Focus on your goals and objectives. Use them to get done what the church needs to get done. Anticipate their needs so that—

MARK (*interrupting*): So that we walk around the elephant in the sanctuary?

BISHOP (*now speaking emphatically*): That elephant happens to be their personality—*who they are!*

LUCY (*even more emphatically*): That elephant is no more who they are than diarrhea and vomit are signs of personality!

BISHOP: What?

MARK: What we are seeing is the symptoms of illness, not personality. We serve a sick church, a highly reactive church, an unsafe church that is spontaneously and unpredictably odd.

LUCY: And whenever we gather together, it's never to ask the Lord's blessing.

BISHOP (*angry*): And who chose you—both of you—to pass judgment on them? Stop diagnosing and start preaching the

Word! Surrender your egos and do the work you were called to do!

LUCY AND MARK (*looking directly at each other*): He saw John's sign!

BISHOP: Sign? What sign?

MARK: John's sign. It's obvious, posted right on our church door.

BISHOP: What does the sign say?

LUCY: It reads, "Enter at own risk. Park your brains and hearts at the door."

BISHOP (*after a long pause*): I am not amused. If you want some assistance, I'll give you the name of a family-dynamics specialist.

LUCY: You mean the ones who talk about family roles?

MARK: How in the world do you think *that* a family-dynamics specialist could help the church?

BISHOP (*standing*): The family-dynamics counselor is not for the church but for the two of you. Neither of you sees your own roles in this family. You haven't paid attention to their personality, so you both are causing these reactions.

MARK (*standing*): Look, we have a pachyderm parked in the pews—and it's not us!

LUCY (*standing*): My calling is not to walk on eggshells, manipulating and anticipating their every reaction— fearful of waking the elephant.

MARK: And my calling is not to become preoccupied with every word out of their mouths as if I'm the general manager of the universe.

LUCY: If we did that, we would have to switch our profession…

MARK: From pastors to the codependent spouses of alcoholics.

LUCY: And what a boatload of joy that would be!

BISHOP (*long pause, standing*): I've heard enough! You both have my offer (*showing them to the door*), and we are willing to pay for the counseling you both need and deserve. Good Day and may God help you!

Discussion Questions

1. If you are the pastor of a church that was regarded as a mess, chaotic, and screwed up, what are your positive and negative expectations on the responses of your church's hierarchy and bishop?
2. Did the bishop come across with interest and empathy? What seems to be the bishop's over-riding concern? If the over-riding concern of the bishop is for the institution rather than healing the church, does the bishop's reaction to the pastors make sense to you?
3. The bishop is using a number of frameworks to look at the church, the pastors, and the odd relational behavior of the church. What lenses, frameworks, or "rocks" would you use to assess this congregation and why?
4. Are your lenses wide enough to include the possibility of organizational trauma? What about the bishop's lenses? Is your chosen framework helpful in healing trauma, or is it worsening the situation by ascribing blame? Do you think your framework would be useful? If yes, in what ways?

Possible Responses to DQ

1. If I am a pastor of the church, I would have expected the hierarchy and the bishop to at least sincerely listen to the issues raised. Since I am someone from the inside who personally sees and experiences the chaos, I could give more accurate descriptions of the events.

    On the other hand, given the prevailing norm in most churches, the "personality-related" misdiagnosis and the agitated reaction of the bishop is somehow expected. I would also probably expect church hierarchy to give remarks such as to simply let the problem pass or to not make a big issue out of it.

2. Weird at it is, but the bishop seemed to be more interested in Mark and Lucy's "clergy marriage" in their partnership in the Gospel compared to the abnormal church reactions. Based on the conversation, for some reason, the bishop is trying to find all potential explanations aside from the the possiblility of church trauma from years ago.

    Ironically, the bishop did listen but had the solutions ready even before understanding the real problem. The bishop did not know what to do but didn't want to admit it. Therefore, without a diagnosis, the Bishop resorted to "Here Try This" treatment plans. Further, the Bishop was more concerned about the institution than the pastors. The bishop was out of options and needed to ask for help.

3. If I am to look at the case, I may look for a model of diagnosing the problem that could explain the sudden, unexpected behaviors of the church. My first thing to do would be to rule out trauma by doing an historical trauma assessment. This is why doctors do a complete history and physical assessment, because history is the best predictor of personal health. If the diagnosis is trauma that was buried, it should not be too difficult to find if pursued with curiosity. The Biblical Model of the hope of Transforming Trauma is that God used the terrible trauma of the cross, and transformed it, to be the greatest blessing the world has ever seen. The Good News is that God also does the same for all our traumas by transforming them into blessings for the world.

4. I do think that the frameworks or models that I would consider are wide enough to address the real problems of the congregation. Ironically, it seems that the bishop's lenses are wide enough too. However, it seems to have an intentional blind spot that conceals the traumatic event twelve years ago. I consider my lenses to be helpful in healing trauma, whereas the bishop's lenses are inclined to assigning blame to the people of the church.

CHAPTER 3

Help Is Coming!

Have you ever been in a position wherein you know an answer to a persisting problem, yet you don't have the voice to speak up? Or if you have the voice to do so, no one out there is willing to listen. The problem stays and persists, even though you know that there is something you can do about it. If caught in this situation, would you just accept the solution that other people impose, or would you be courageous to pursue your solutions even without their support?

Commentary

Churches that lack the language to describe and make meaning from their trauma become flame-throwing blamers. After all, it is far easier to blame and scapegoat than to admit, "I don't have a clue why we act so strange!" That kind of honesty takes the courage that requires in-depth self-reflection.

However, for post-traumatic congregations, there is no self-reflection because the truth is buried in the backyard. So, who is left to blame for their being cranky, controlling, and numb? Unfortunately, pastoral leadership is always first on the blame list. Instead of the congregation being held accountable and responsible for their misconducts, the system remains untouched because it's far easier to move a pastor than to move a whole congregation. Thus, the current pastors accept the beatings over and over again until the next new pastorate takes their place. And then the blaming and beating cycle continues.

There is a myriad of clergy and church-assessment tools, but not even one is designed to assess trauma. This is in spite of the fact that if the trauma is not assessed *first*, all the other assessments will be flat-out skewed and dead wrong. Ask whether there are post-trauma fighters, fliers, and freezers in the house? If so, make a trauma history *first* before doing a ton of other assessments that will only lead down a maze of rabbit holes.

If people are continually on guard, holding their breath while carefully stepping around elephants and golden calves, don't you think it is just appropriate to look under the trauma rock?

If people are self-censoring and unable to speak honestly, doesn't the trauma rock has the answer?

If people are busy being politically correct instead of self-disclosing, then again, the thing under the trauma rock is probably messing things up.

Interestingly, the bishop looked under all the rocks but one— the trauma rock. When congregational communication becomes politicized, why is it so difficult to ask, "When did it get so toxic?" "What happened to make it toxic?" and "Where is the trauma?"

Surprisingly, those questions never get asked, and so they get buried, stepped around, and then we pretend they never happened nor existed in the first place.

Looking closer, it can be seen that three dysfunctional family rules prevent the discovery of trauma:

(1) don't talk about it,
(2) don't feel anything about it, and
(3) don't trust anyone with it.

People adapt to the rules by taking on the five roles of a codependent family. Sadly, the pastor is assigned with the caretaker role, running around and taking care of everyone instead of modeling and empowering each family member for healing self-care.

Therefore, ignoring the appropriate trauma questions pre-disposes clergy to codependency through centralized power and top-down unilateral decision-making structures to control the post-traumatic sheep. Consequently, the spiritual empowerment of the sheep is sacrificed and compromised. Creative, logical, empathetic thinking is replaced by disinterested, belligerent ignorance. Instead of directly addressing trauma, we cut off our nose to spite our face.

The bishop asked questions on organizational development and faithfulness to the gospel. The bishop also asked whether the staff had interpersonal-relationship or staff-development issues. However, regardless if intentional or unintentional, the bishop ignored asking questions related to trauma. This exposed the church to a catchall conclusion, an irrelevant diagnosis,

"We could not definitively find the problem, so we concluded it must be the church's personality, so, Here Try This!"

Such diagnosis is not only unhelpful but is also detrimental to the health of the church. Uneducated guessing hinders curiosity and investigation, leaving the church hopeless for healing and growth.

Traumatized churches are often misdiagnosed as "having a personality disorder." Being diagnosed as such leaves clergy with only three options. First, they can choose to be a flier and leave. They can also opt to be freezers, ignoring the situation as if nothing is happening. Finally, the clergy can be a fighter, trying to control the institution despite its unhealthy state.

None of the three options is healthy. They all enable the problem to continue matastasizing. In short, misdiagnosis caused by asking the wrong questions or by not asking the right questions only make the sick even sicker.

In simpler words, this enabling stance of lay pastoral leadership can be described as "handling people with kid gloves, walking on eggshells, stepping around the elephant, or holding our breath." None of these is good, and it all yields to the same bad fruit. The bad fruit that keeps prisoners unfree, further blinds those unable to see, and causes difficulty for lame to walk. The dead cannot be raised because of the breath of life that resurrects health is missing in the first place.

Enabling church leadership is neither empowering nor faithful. The Traumatized One's proclamation of the good news of post-trauma life and growth cannot be lived up because, instead of lifting up the trauma to the cross, we hide it. We ignore it. We pray to God that it spontaneously goes away. And when all else fails, we attempt to control it and thereby encouraging its continuance, even unto the third and fourth generations.

When a church has been traumatized, its foundations have also been damaged and compromised. This damage requires the congregation to develop words, a language, and multiple conversations to assess the damage and communicate the needs. Foundational repairs need to be negotiated with knowledge, creativity, and compassion to ensure the safety and healing of the community.

Educational and debriefing structures are helpful in communally processing the trauma. These can encourage people to help one another in bringing trauma to its simplest forms. For example, you are a farmer. You have lots of branches laid in your backyard. You know the branches are useful, but they cannot be put into any use until you process them. In this example, the farmer needs to use a wood chipper to turn the branches into mulch. Only then can the branches be of significant use to the farmer and his farm. Educational and debriefing structures work the same. Trauma will never be beneficial unless it is processed accordingly. For a traumatized church, the resulting mulch can be likened to the *lessons learned from the trauma*. These learnings can serve as a guide in making decisions for your life and for growth.

By living on the learnings from the trauma, you can be a living testament that God's goodness can heal all. Besides, based on the healing ministry of Jesus, it is apparent what God's will is. That is for the traumatized to become thrivers, to have life, and to have it abundantly.

Like how the foundations of your houses work, a wounded and damaged community's foundation cannot be repaired through quick fixes. It cannot be corrected through renovations or repainting. What it needs is security, to make the foundations stable and firm once again. After all, a foolish man builds his house upon the sand, but a wise man builds his upon a rock.

Trauma damages foundations. So, why aren't we looking under the trauma rock *first*?

Reader's Theatre

Act 1, Scene 3: The Morning-After Breakfast

Mark, Lucy, and John are having breakfast in a fast-food restaurant. John is the last one to get his food. He sits at the table where Lucy and Mark are seated, but notices Lucy does not have any food.

JOHN: Lucy, I thought you were eating.
LUCY: I did.
JOHN: You mean, you're done? Already?
MARK: I told you, when it comes to eating, she's greased lightning.
LUCY: *Without* the grease! I've just always eaten this way—habit, I guess. But do you want to know about the bishop's meeting?
JOHN: Yeah! (*looking at both them and pausing*) Well?
LUCY: I'm sorry to report (*pausing*)...nothing good came out of Jerusalem!
JOHN: Oh no.
MARK: Oh yes. (*Speaking in pulpit tones, he continues.*) We are gathered here today to say good-bye to our clergy careers...
JOHN: What do you mean? What happened?
LUCY: It didn't go well.
MARK: The bishop asked us about our relationship, how we get along and how we work together...questioning our styles...
LUCY: And even our sense of humor. Can you imagine that!
JOHN: Well, the two of you are...outrageous.
MARK: You're right, we are. But it felt strange, like I was getting backed into a corner, almost like...like I was going down... down into the church's crawl space.

Healing Traumatized Churches

Bringing the Traumatized into the Revelation

Pastor Ronald H. Wean
M.Div., M.Ed., LPCC

Founder: HTC Ministries, LLC

Pastor Mighty Fortress Lutheran Church

625 Cherry Blossom Drive, Dayton, Ohio, 45449

www.htcministry.com

rwean@sbcglobal.net

937 361 2073

Healing Traumatized Churches

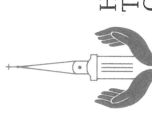

Healing Traumatized Churches

Transforming the Traumatized into the Revitalized

LUCY: Now that's my job. Will crawl for food!

MARK: The job is yours, 'cause I'm not going down there. But it felt like I was down there…in the bishop's office…trapped. And then the bishop ended the meeting.

LUCY: Thank God!

MARK: The bishop ended it with recommendations to consult with a family- dynamics specialist.

JOHN: A what? A family-dynamics specialist? But why? What good is a family- dynamics specialist?

LUCY: To identify what roles we played in our family? Go figure! When you only have a hammer in the toolbox, you just see nails and nothing else. But the meeting just went south—and quick.

JOHN: Well, it could have gone worse.

LUCY AND MARK: Worse?

MARK: How could it have gone any worse?

JOHN: You could have gotten *the stare*!

LUCY AND MARK: The stare?

LUCY (*pausing*): You mean the "you have three noses on your face" stare?

JOHN: That's the one—*the stare*.

MARK: I'm afraid we got *the stare* when we mentioned your sign.

JOHN: *My sign*? How did I get into this? I wasn't there! What sign?

LUCY: Your sign—your "Enter at own risk. Park your brains and hearts at the door" sign.

JOHN: Oh, *that* sign.

LUCY: And it was not pretty!

MARK: But I also got *the glare*.

JOHN (*in horror*): The glare? You got *the stare* and *the glare*?

LUCY: I got a piece of that, too…when the bishop diagnosed the church with a personality problem.

MARK: And Lucy objected, saying the diagnosis of personality was like using the flu symptoms of vomit and diarrhea and calling them signs of a personality disorder!

JOHN (*to Lucy*): You didn't!

LUCY: I did.

JOHN: Why would you say that to a…to a—

MARK (*interrupting*): But *the glare* was there when I refused to be a codependent spouse of an alcoholic.

JOHN: A what?

MARK: A codependent spouse of an alcoholic, the non-drinking spouse in an alcoholic family whose focus is on everyone's needs but their own.

LUCY: They enable the sick to stay sick by burying the family mess just to keep the ship afloat…

MARK: Even though it's already the *Titanic*!

MARK: Codependent spouses are resentful and angry. Controlling and manipulating everyone and everything.

LUCY: And that ain't pretty! But many people believe that good pastors act a lot like the spouses of alcoholics.

MARK: In fact, an old Chicago clergy study even discovered that 80 percent of the Chicago-land clergy were children of alcoholics.

LUCY: And 95 percent of trauma nurses were firstborn children of alcoholics!

JOHN: Huh, so the children are codependents in training?

MARK: My guess is that those vocations are attractive to adult children of alcoholics because they have learned to keep on keepin' on despite the ongoing family trauma and chaos.

LUCY: It just feels normal to have blood and guts all over the place at the office. To them, it's just another day at home!

JOHN: Well, if you two ever become codependent, I know what your first casualty would be.

MARK AND LUCY: What's that? Tell us! What?

JOHN: Your sense of humor.

MARK (*laughing*): Fat chance!

LUCY (*sarcastically, with a fake Southern-belle accent*): Oh Mark, you know the bishop…the bishop…just loves to love everybody. Why the Bishop just can't wait to see little old us again!

JOHN: Wait, the bishop can't fire you, can he?

MARK: Nope,can't do that anymore. Ever sincethemerger, the bishop lost the power to fire anybody.

LUCY: In fact, the bishop can't do a whole lot unless invited in by most of the church council. But even then, the bishop can only recommend.

JOHN: But what if the pastor is the problem? What happens to the church then?

MARK AND LUCY (*looking at each other*): They are so-o-o screwed!

JOHN (*thoughtfully pausing*): I don't want to be ordained.

LUCY: Oh John, now where's *your* sense of humor?

JOHN: I don't want to be ordained to an organization that has no partnership, no…eh…eh…

MARK: Accountability?

JOHN: Accountability! But no mutual accountability? How in the world did that happen?

LUCY: Don't know exactly, but there were three church bodies that merged. Each was the exact same denomination. Just three different histories, three different cultures, three…

MARK: Three different flavors of the same thing! And instead of the three taking the time to negotiate for consensus, they took a shortcut and voted—just get married. It's like politicians passing bills and saying, "We passed the bill to find out what's in it!"

JOHN: Oh, I see… So, we discovered we had lost our Bishops *after* the marriage?

LUCY: And then we learned that there was no bishop, no partnership, and no room in the inn of accountability! You are out there on your own, stuck with a franchise.

MARK: Each church is now totally autonomous. There is no outside accountability. It's now easy pickings for every narcissist, every control freak, and every snake charmer coming down the pike.

LUCY: So-o-o, John, that's why we want you to be ordained.

JOHN: Wait a minute! Are you calling me a narcissistic control-freak snake charmer?

LUCY: Well, if the shoe fits…(*pausing*)

LUCY: No, silly! You…you have a conscience. Narcissists don't. You actually care about the people in church. That's why you're so bothered by these exploding meetings.

MARK: The world is full of ordained narcissists and codependents. What we need is someone called…called…with a conscience.

LUCY: Called with a conscience? Oh my! That one deserves top billing.(as if reading poetry) Called with a conscience…call Pastor Mark. He is the one…called with a conscience!

MARK: Called with a conscience—to care for the sheep! And so it's you, John.

LUCY: Consider yourself called to come with us to the conference.

JOHN: To the conference? What conference? (*looking at them*) You two are serious? I mean, this is not one of your jokes, is it?

LUCY: On occasion we can be serious. But then we feel so-o-o-o guilty!

JOHN: So you are joking.

LUCY AND MARK: Absolutely not!

LUCY: You're coming with us to a conference on healing.

MARK: Healing Traumatized Churches—it might explain our mystery.

JOHN (*interjecting questions*): What? When? Who is going to be there? What's this about?

LUCY: The bishop didn't want to go, especially with us. So you're it!

MARK: Consider this your first call. We found this conference on the Internet…

LUCY: And the description of a church in post-trauma reaction. It sounds a lot like our church. The sudden odd reactions…

MARK: The lack of energy for anything, except for being cranky and controlling…

LUCY: The attempts to ignore the parked pachyderms in the sanctuary!

JOHN: Wait! Now you didn't say that to the…to the…

LUCY: To the bishop? Of course I did not say that to the bishop.

MARK (*pausing*): I did!

JOHN: You've got to be out of your…

LUCY: That one got us *the glare*! (*She gives an exaggerated glare at both Mark and John.*)

JOHN: Oh no!

LUCY (*continuing the glare toward John*): And you will go with us to the conference, and you will like it!

MARK: Go home and think about it. Talk to Maggie about coming with us.

JOHN: That's not fair.

MARK: Why is talking to Maggie not fair? She's your wife.

JOHN: Have you talked with her?

MARK: No. What's wrong?

JOHN: Well, nothing's wrong. She just has been telling me the same things, that I should consider a…a career change…to the ministry.

LUCY: Hallelujah and praise Jesus for spouses! Thank God for Maggie!

MARK: So great minds and the Holy Spirit think alike. Talk to Maggie, and then let's get ready to rumble!

LUCY (*singing*): Pack up the babies and grab the old ladies to Brother Love's song! You're coming to the conference!

JOHN: What in the world have I gotten into?

Discussion Questions

1. Both Pastors insist that John has a "call" to go to the Healing Traumatized Churches Workshop. This "call" also seems to be confirmed by John's spouse. Is this the way God calls people? How has God called you?

2. How would you describe the relationship between John, Lucy, and Mark? Is it healthy or unhealthy? What makes it either one? Would you feel comfortable talking to these three? Do the two pastors conform to your image of being pastors? Do they conform to the bishop's expectations of what a pastor does?

3. How tolerant is your pastor, church authority, or church hierarchy to questions, push back, and humor? Is there a connection between health and pushing back questioning, and humor?

4. What has happened to you when you have questioned, pushed back, or used humor in the church? In your church's history, what healing plan was put forward to directly address and actually heal the trauma?

Possible Responses to DQ

1. There are a variety of ways on how God calls people to be an ambassador for Christ. One must be caring. Loving. Forgiving. To be a vehicle for healing. Like John, you have to bloom where you are planted!

    His church's trauma, as exhibited every church meeting, must be God's way of calling John. Of all the people in the congregation, only he has the interest and courage to question and look deeper into the problem.

2. The relationship between Mark, Lucy, and John is healthy. They can freely talk about the matters of the church. They can raise the question and incorporate humor in their discussions. They were also supportive of each other and productively discuss the real issues without resorting to the generic responses and blame game.

    Mark and Lucy conform to God's image of pastors. Instead of burying, they promote healing in the church. They hope to relieve the congregation of its trauma so that it can fulfill its role of stewardship and sharing of the Gospel positively and productively. However, Mark and Lucy do not conform to the Bishop's image of a pastor. The Bishop expects the two to be passive of the issue and simply accept the solutions being offered. The Bishop expected the pastors to simply bury the trauma by looking under the other rocks, without questions asked.

3. I don't think any authority wants to be questioned because authority takes itself way too seriously. Sometimes, a taste of power kills off common sense; other times, the willingness to understand the situation is the one that is killed.

The people in the kingdom knew that the emperor has no clothes! The story of the emperor is a clear example of the danger of disguising ignorance as knowledge. Besides, asking for help is a great sign of leadership.

CHAPTER 4:

The Eye-Opening

Imagine living in a lawless community. With everyone free and vulnerable at the same time, what kind of people would you expect to be fond of such a community. Would the innocent and soft-hearted people prevail? Or would the extremists and opportunists take advantage of the place's lawlessness and lack of accountability and responsibility?

Commentary

The previous scene described an organization where the relationship of the local church and the middle governing body is inadequately explained. The role of the bishop, the judicatory leader, is not clearly assigned. As a result, the congregations nor the pastors cannot be held accountable for their words and actions simply because no office was given the authority to do so. This is a common mistake among judicatories regardless if they are bishop-led or not.

The lack of clarity and accountability in an organization is not only nonsense, but it is also quite dangerous to the entire system. In an organization like this, the "narcissist control-freak snake charmers" get free passes to devour the sheep. No one in authority can intervene nor offer assistance to the traumatized churches and their serving pastors. The lack of safeguards—transparency, accountability, and mutual partnership welcomes personalities with personal agendas with open arms. This system also becomes attractive to those pastors and lay codependent leaders. These people excel in controlling other people's reactions and awareness with band-aid solutions. Codependent leadership enjoys walking on eggshells and handling everyone with kid gloves just to control the reactivity of the congregation. Obviously, this ministry model enables unhealthy, reactive systems to continue, impeding both honest trauma conversations as well as the mission of the church.

Therefore, the lack of clearly stated authoritative role and function within the community of congregations leaves an open door for traumatic church local leaders. This structure welcomes lay and clergy that are either narcissistic, codependent or simply control freaks.

A system without transparency and accountability looks odd and nonsensical. It does not foster creativity, logic, and faith. When a congregation or pastor is operating independently of the wider faith community, the grim biblical description becomes a reality, "Each one does what is right in his own eyes."

With this reality as clear as the sky, why would anyone intentionally omit the important role of the bishop and other judicatory bodies? Could it be another result of post-trauma? Are they guilty of traumatizing flocks through the abuse of power? It wouldn't hurt to look at history. Identify the trauma events, and ask, "Was this trauma ever debriefed, processed, or mulched into learning? Or was it simply buried?"

Why is there a struggle to raising trauma questions? Why are we so afraid to investigate? Why do we refuse to look under the trauma rock?

Look and then ask if the trauma was ever debriefed, processed, or integrated into the awareness of the congregation. Was it even mentioned in the first place?

If your investigation leads you to the conclusion that "people just forgot about it because time heals all wounds" or "people never brought it up, so we thought everything was okay," then know that your evidence is still alive and kicking. Look in the backyard for the collective spiritual toxic waste sites. It's all right there, buried and sinking deeper into the congregation's psyche. It is poisoning the human ecology and siphoning the strength and vitality of the congregation's breath.

Even a simple trauma assessment on such an illogical organizational design would quickly reveal whether its flaws come from post-trauma reaction. The problem is that assessment itself seldom happens.

If indeed there was a buried trauma, it could well explain the absence of safeguards and structures between the bishop and judicatory structure. However, without the words, language, and a trauma framework, no one would dare ask whether the bishop's office was dismantled as a result of a post-trauma reaction. Unfortunately, not asking the question leaves congregations at risk from inside and out.

Reader's Theatre

Act 1, Scene 4: The Keynote Conference Speaker

Mark, Lucy, and John are rushing toward an open table to take their seats. The conference is about to begin.

JOHN: We finally made it! But I got a question.
MARK AND LUCY: What's that?
JOHN: Half my breakfast is still making its way down. How can you possibly eat that fast?
LUCY: Practice, practice, and more practice!
MARK: You'll get used to it, John. And again, I really appreciate you coming with us.
LUCY: So do I. Just wouldn't be the same without you!
JOHN: Well, I still don't know how you talked me into this. All these clergy collars (*looking around*) everywhere. It's like a...a monastery or something.
MARK: Welcome to the club!
LUCY: And all this could be yours, John.
JOHN: No way!

ANNOUNCER: The conference "Healing Traumatized Churches" is about to begin. Please take your seats. We will begin shortly.

JOHN: I brought you both something, a little token of myesteem, my admiration, my gratitude, my...

MARK: My, oh my, oh my!

JOHN: Well...here! (*He hands out packages.*) Gifts from me to you.

LUCY: Should we beware of Greeks bearing gifts?

JOHN: Ha! No, it's a memento of our times together. Here! Open them.

MARK (*opening the package*): You got us our very own...sign?

LUCY (*She takes her sign out, then holds it up and reads it*): Enter at own risk. Park your brains and hearts at the door.

MARK: Now you truly are one of us.

LUCY: Somebody, go get him a collar!

JOHN: I'm out of here! (*Both Mark and Lucy grab John's arms and lead him in.*)

As the three of them get situated, the speaker begins.

SPEAKER: Welcome to this first conference on healing church trauma. I personally wish to thank you all for coming. You are all brave enough not to have run in the other direction when you heard the word *trauma*. But like emergency and fire personnel, you chose to run*toward* a burning church, and that is for a greater good.

JOHN (*whispering*): Nuts! Now I really want to leave!

LUCY (*whispering*): You can't go, or I'll nail your other foot to the floor!

MARK (*whispering*): Trust me! We'll tell you when the building is on fire!

JOHN: Joking, always joking. Jokes, jokes, and more— MARK AND LUCY: Shh-h-h-h!

SPEAKER: You are all brave to come to this conference, a conference that combines the words *church* and *trauma*. For many people, those words are an oxymoron—like "jumbo shrimp" I must say. They just don't fit together. But they do fit! In fact, they are stuck together from the very beginning. That is because the ancient symbol for trauma is also the ancient symbol of the church. (*He pauses.*) Anyone know this ancient symbol?

AUDIENCE MEMBER (*yelling*): The fish?

SPEAKER: The fish is a good symbol, but not the universal symbol for the church. Anyone else?

ANOTHER AUDIENCE MEMBER (*yelling*): The cross!

SPEAKER: Yes! The ancient symbol for trauma became the symbol for the church, and it happened even *without* the trauma conversation.

Everyone here follows the Traumatized One. But in our churches, we still don't talk about trauma. We commemorate the Palm Sunday and briefly add Good Friday at the very end of the Palm Sunday Service. But next Sunday on Easter, we go directly to the resurrection, skipping over Good Friday and the crucifixion! How convenient that we would go from the victorious ride into Jersusalem on Palm Sunday to His Victory on Easter Sunday, excluding the bloody cross! So how come? How come we church people go out of our way *not* to talk about the trauma of Good Friday? Any ideas?

LUCY: It's against the rules. (*Both Mark and John perk up and look at Lucy; the audience reacts with silence.*)

SPEAKER: Against the rules? What rules do you mean?

LUCY: The rules say the church must be a happy place. (*The audience laughs nervously, nodding.*)

SPEAKER (*pausing*): Oh-h-h, those rules! Anyone ever heard of those rules?

(*Most of the audience raises their hands.*)

SPEAKER: So, you all are here…breaking all the rules. What an excitement!

LUCY: There will be…when I get reimbursed! (*The audience laughs.*)

SPEAKER (*pausing for audience*): Do I know you?

LUCY: Nope! I'm Lucy, Lucy from Michigan! (*There are a few cheers, and Lucy waves.*)

SPEAKER: So-o-o, Lucy from Michigan, you are…a Wolverine! (*The audience laughs.*)

LUCY: Yep—and proud of it! (*some oohs*)

SPEAKER (*singing softly into the mike*): I don't give a darn for the whole state of Michigan, the whole state of Michigan, the whole state of Michigan… (*The audience starts to really laugh; Lucy laughs too.*)

SPEAKER (*as the laughter dies down*): This might be the first church trauma conference where people do have some fun! Thank you, again, for coming. You are brave to break the rules and connect trauma and healing in the church. (*He pauses.*)

We are all here because of a man named Viktor Frankl. Viktor Frankl was a concentration-camp survivor, surviving the horrors of Auschwitz.

In his book *Man's Search for Meaning*, we see that Viktor survived because he had *words*. He had words, language, and a framework to make meaning out of the total darkness around him. And because he had language, because he had *words,* he survived.

He survived because through language, he could process the trauma that surrounded him, that filled his nostrils, and died next to him. He survived because

words stimulated his brain to find meaning in the trauma of the evil drama. He survived because he did not bury the experience in forgotten memory. Instead, he learned from it.

Because he chose not to be silent and decided not to put his mind to sleep, Viktor became the brightest student of the darkest trauma. So today, as we begin our journey into church healing, we will remember Viktor Frankl as the Father of Trauma Healing. And today, our first step toward understanding church trauma is the same first step taken by Viktor Frankl himself—to develop a language to describe our own trauma.

In order to understand trauma, we need to know how the brain works. From the PowerPoint, you can see that with language, the brain works like a wood chipper. Now how many of you have worked with one of those things? (*He looks over the audience at a few hands going up.*) What's the best thing about using a wood chipper?

AUDIENCE MEMBER: You get mulch for growing things!

SPEAKER: Yes! When you put stuff in a wood chipper, you get mulch. And if you can't use it all in the garden, you can store it in the barn for future use, like for making your future plants grow. But what happens if you throw a log that's too big into that wood chipper?

ANOTHER AUDIENCE MEMBER: It gets jammed—shuts down.

SPEAKER: Yes, jammed and shut down. So how do you unjam a jammed wood chipper?

LUCY (*yelling out*): Dynamite! (*The audience laughs.*)

MARK AND JOHN (*leaning over, whispering*): Lu-u-c-c-y-y?

LUCY: I'm answering the question!

SPEAKER (*laughing*): Just call Lucy the Wolverine. She will fix anything! (*He pauses for the audience.*) But…but the brain does work like a wood chipper. The brain also takes in the stuff of life and processes them. Using words, it grinds the stuff up and turn them into mulch or the *learning* as we still call it. And that learning is stored in our memory, our barn, to be used in making future decisions for life and growth.

But like a wood chipper, big logs can jam the brain. The brain can't mulch that much information because the information is just too big, too large, too much to process. These logs—too big for our brains to process—overwhelm us…these logs are called "*trauma.*"

The trauma logs jam us up. Our brains shut down, and we're just plain stuck. And we hate it! We hate it because being jammed up makes us feel powerless, vulnerable. Like we are losing control. And so, it terrifies us. It just scares us to death.

So-o-o, just like the jammed wood chipper, the big log of trauma must get dislodged. But how do we unjam a stuck brain?

AUDIENCE MEMBER: Blow it up! (*The audience laughs.*)

SPEAKER (*pausing*): Are you from Michigan too? (*more laughter*) Well, some people do blow up, but does that work? Others just freeze up like deer in headlights. And still others choose to run.

Those fight, flight, and freeze survival reactions come from the lower part of the brain. However, they don't solve the problem because the jammed processor is in the upper part of the brain.

The good news is that it can be unjammed! It can be done *with the help of other people*, people brave enough to talk. The people who know how to use the brain's natural unjammer—*words*. Words!

Words that validate. Words that normalize the terrified. Words that give hope. Through sharing our own trauma experiences, our brains just light up with connection to others *through words*. Our brains love words.

Having the *words of trauma* gives us a shared framework, a unity, a healing and *trauma conversation*. It gives us connection, a connection to help each other.

Now, how do you think conversations with others process trauma?

LUCY: Two heads are better than one.

SPEAKER: Lucy, you hit the nail on the head! (*The audience groans.*) Okay, my kids don't think I'm funny, either. (*The audience chuckles.*) But Lucy is right. If thetrauma is too big for one wood chipper, a few more talking heads can mulch it down to size. (*The audience groans again.*)

This help from others is called *critical-stress debriefing*. How many of you have ever heard of or attended a critical-stress debriefing? (*He waits, but only three hands are raised.*)

Debriefings occur following trauma. They are successful when people feel *safe*—safe enough to speak words *freely*.

Only when people feel safe and speak freely can brains unjam to process the trauma.

Now, how many of you have ever attended a critical-incident debriefing in your church?

JOHN (*raising his hand*): They called it that, but it wasn't safe, not safe enough for anyone to speak.

SPEAKER: What do you mean, it wasn't safe?

JOHN: The bishop came and told us it was God's will to forgive and forget. After that, we just worried that we would be seen as unfaithful if we talked about it. It wasn't safe; and so nobody talked.

SPEAKER: You were left with some thoughts? Thoughts that bothered you?

JOHN (*forcefully*): Yeah, I had plenty of thoughts. I just hoped I wouldn't run into him (*pounding one fist into the other*)...at the grocery store. (*The audience breaks out in nervous laughter.*)

SPEAKER: The bishop or the pastor?

JOHN: Both! (*The audience again breaks out in nervous laughter.*)

SPEAKER (*pausing*): Still hoping?

JOHN (*looking around, down*): Yeah. It's been twelve years. It still... still could get ugly.

SPEAKER: Thank you for your honesty. And your name?

JOHN: I'm John.

SPEAKER: Are you from Michigan? (*The audience laughs.*)

JOHN: No. I'm from the great state of Wisconsin! (*The audience responds, "Wo-oo-oo!"*)

SPEAKER: So! You're a Badger?

JOHN: One hundred percent! (*The audience chuckles.*)

SPEAKER: Now, how can a Badger sit at the same table with a Wolverine? (*The audience chuckles again.*)

LUCY (*singing*): It's the p-p-power of love! (*The audience laughs.*)

SPEAKER: So, this really is The *I Love Lucy* show! (*The audience groans.*)

AUDIENCE MEMBER: Your kids are right! (*The audience laughs.*)

SPEAKER (*waiting for audience*): By everyone's reaction today, they are. But getting back to what John shared, he still wonders what he would do if he ran into them at the grocery store—even twelve years later. Anyone care to make sense out of that?

FIRST AUDIENCE MEMBER: He's holding a grudge? SPEAKER: Holding a grudge. Anyone else? SECOND AUDIENCE MEMBER: He can't let it go?

SPEAKER: He can't let go…of what? What does he need to let go of?

THIRD AUDIENCE MEMBER: He can't let go of the past? SPEAKER: How would he do that?

FIRST AUDIENCE MEMBER: Just forget about it and move on! SPEAKER: He tried that already. Didn't you, John?

JOHN: Yeah, it didn't work.

SPEAKER: Is that why you're here?

JOHN: No.

SPEAKER: Then why did you come?

JOHN: I came to this conference kicking and screaming because I knew I'd have to stop—to stop trying to bury it, to face it instead of being so angry…so (*realization dawning*)…so cranky and controlling. Every time I think about it, I get cranky and controlling.

SPEAKER (*long pause*): Again, thank you for your honesty, John. What John described is a fight reaction. It is a survival reaction, a normal post-trauma reaction that could be triggered by either the traumatizer or someone quoting the traumatizer. It can also be unleashed by a similar feeling about the traumatizer, or feelings of powerlessness, vulnerability, and loss of control.

JOHN: You mean I'm stuck with this for the rest of my life?

SPEAKER: No, it just means the stuck log never got processed, never got turned into mulch.

JOHN: Well, where did it go?

SPEAKER: Into memory.

JOHN: How?

SPEAKER: The trauma log gets chucked out of the processor and thrown into memory. And there it sits—unprocessed, un-debriefed, and unavailable for future decision- making. It just sits in the backyard of memory.

It's buried in the backyard of memory, covered over with burial words— words like:

"Let's just move on."

"We don't have to talk about it anymore."

"What's done is done."

"It is what it is."

The trauma burial even receives the bishop's final benedictory words, that "God's will is that you forgive and forget."

So there, it just sits—sits and waits to be triggered.

AUDIENCE MEMBER: What do you mean, "triggered"?

SPEAKER: The trauma event is still full of energy—the energy from terror, the energy from being powerless and vulnerable, the energy from losing control, the energy of self-blame.

AUDIENCE MEMBER: What self-blame? Trauma is something that just happens. It happens suddenly and unexpectedly, and people just get overwhelmed. So why blame yourself?

SPEAKER: Good question. Anybody have any ideas?

LUCY: Monday morning quarterbacking! (*The audience nervously laughs.*)

MARK (*whispering*): You are in rare form.

LUCY (*whispering back*): I'm just getting started.

JOHN (*whispering back*): It's the Lucy show!

SPEAKER: Great observation! We all hate being powerless, losing control, and being vulnerable. So when trauma happens to us, we all become Monday morning quarterbacks.

We "woulda-coulda-shoulda" ourselves to death, denying the reality that trauma happened and thinking somehow we should have prevented it, could have stopped it, or somehow controlled the outcome.

Therefore, the large, jammed log of unprocessed trauma, soaked in "woulda-coulda-shoulda" and buried with tons of "get over it, just move on,forgive and forget, and we don't have to talk about this" just becomes a toxic waste site in the backyard of our mind.

LUCY: What a lovely image! (*The audience laughs.*)

SPEAKER (*also laughs*): Right. As my kids would say, "Real yucky!" So, what's in your backyard? What double, double toil and trouble have you been brewing, accumulating, marinating in that precious mind of yours?

Today's exercise is designed to take a look at the backyard, to get a glimpse of those mental toxic sites.

Therefore, please divide into groups of three. And after you secure your threesome, take a few minutes to introduce yourselves and tell why you came. Then make a group decision about which one will be the first *speaker*, the first *listener*, and the first *observer*. Every one of you will have the opportunity to do each of the roles when we rotate. So please, find your threesome.

JOHN: What did you two get me into? Good God!

LUCY: I couldn't agree more!

JOHN: Agree with what?

LUCY: The part about God being good. I wholeheartedly agree.

MARK: So, do we have a threesome, or should we look for another?

LUCY: You're stuck with us. (*Then she looks at John.*) And John, you can run, but you can't hide. So, knock off eyeballing that exit sign!

JOHN: Lucy, to whom shall we go? You have the words of eternal life!

LUCY: Oooo, touché. Way to go!

MARK: Good one, John. Now who wants to be the...the...

LUCY: The speaker, the listener, and the observer.

JOHN: I'll be the observer.

LUCY: Chick-chick-chick-chickee-ee-ee!

MARK: There's that giant chicken sound again.

JOHN: Look, I'm the amateur. And besides, *you* invited *me*, remember?

MARK: Okay, okay. And I'll be the listener.

LUCY: Oh, that's a first! Ladies first, huh?

MARK: Whining will get you everywhere!

SPEAKER: Thank you for getting into your groups of three. Now let us begin. Your first assignment is to identify anything odd that you do, out of character, or even weird or embarrassing. Share it with the listener and observer. Take five minutes and tell what happens, what it's been like for you, and how you cope with it.

Are there any questions? All right. Take a minute to get situated, and we will begin shortly (*Chairs are moved for the three to face each other. The noise stops.*) You may begin—now!

LUCY (*looking at Mark*): Well, since you guys elected me the first woman, let's go. But you both know what I'm going to say.

MARK: No, I don't.

JOHN (*looking at Lucy*): I've got no clue. Oops! I'm the observer. I need to quiet.

LUCY: You don't know? It's so obvious, especially with you two geniuses. We talk about it all the time.

MARK: We do?

LUCY: It's so…obvious, so embarrassing.

MARK: What is it? Please, tell us.

LUCY: It's my fast eating. It's terrible! I can't slow down. Even when I try, I just get so nervous. (*She looks down.*)

MARK (*confused*): I'm shocked. You seem to joke about it all the time.

LUCY: Yeah, I know: "greased lightning without the grease". My humor hides my embarrassment whenever someone says,

"My, you eat fast," or
"Your food just disappeared," or
"There is no need to rush."

I could just die! No matter what I've tried, I'm still gulping it down like my life depended on it (*tears beginning to form*)…and I don't know why.

MARK: I'm so sorry. I never meant to hurt you when I joked about…

LUCY: Please don't apologize. Your acceptance of me far outweighs the banter about the speed of my fork.

MARK: Doing it again? Using humor to hide?

LUCY: See what I mean? It's so natural—using humor—to cover it up and bury it. It bothers me so much, so why do I do it? It's just so, so weird. I even went to counseling.

MARK: You did? When?

LUCY: A couple of years before becoming a pastor. The counselor was nice, someone listening and accepting me. But it didn't work. Just when we thought we had it licked, with all those good thoughts and affirmations, suddenly—oops! I'd be on automatic pilot again, gulping everything down like I was going to a fire.

MARK: It must be hard for you.

LUCY: But only when I forget to chew!

MARK: Bada bing, bada boom! Humor—again and again.

LUCY: Yeah, I know. I just like eating fast…served with a side order of humor.

SPEAKER: Time's up. Now rotate the roles. The speaker can switch to the observer, the observer to the listener, and the listener to the speaker. It will help change your roles to switch your seats. (*The speaker waits.*) You may begin—now!

MARK (*looking at Lucy*): Well, now that you showed me yours, I'll show you mine. (*Now he looks at John.*) But you both know it already. It's also really quite obvious.

JOHN: Well, it's not obvious to me, so I guess I'm no genius.

MARK: It's just that…well… I've joked about it and even used Lucy's food thing to cover it up.

JOHN (*encouragingly*): Markust us.

MARK: Okay, here it goes. It's small spaces, dark places.

JOHN: The what?

MARK: Small spaces, dark places. I just freak out! So, I avoid them like the plague. I even buy breakfast for Lucy to avoid going down into the church crawl space 'cause I definitely won't go down there.

LUCY: Will crawl for food!

JOHN: Lucy, you're funny, but you are the observer.

LUCY: Oops. Sorry.

MARK (*looking at Lucy*): Oh, no problem. Your humor—it always brings me out of my funk.

JOHN: You? You get into…funks?

MARK: Yeah. Whenever I feel like I'm backed into a dark place or feel like I'm trapped, *funk happens*. When we were in the bishop's office, when he didn't listen, that's when I got into my funk. It's better than going ballistic and making a fool out of myself.

JOHN: Good, God! That's what I say to Maggie whenever I get into my own funks. (*He speaks again as realization dawns.*) Oops, sorry. I'm the listener.

MARK: No, don't be, 'cause that was helpful. I thought I was the only one who got into funks. No wonder I've always liked you, John.

JOHN: You like me because we're both funky?

LUCY (*pausing*): I hate to interrupt this funky meeting, but…

SPEAKER: Time is up.

LUCY: Aw-w-w, saved by the bell.

SPEAKER: Again, please rotate so that you play your last role. (*He waits for them to switch chairs.*) You may begin.

MARK: I get to observe.

LUCY: I'll give listening a shot.

JOHN: And I guess I'm up.

LUCY: Sort of like hear no evil, see no evil, speak—

JOHN (*interrupting*): Lucy, I'm nervous as it is, so please be my listener, and not my stand-up.

LUCY: Oops. Sorry…again.

JOHN: I know. And you are hysterical. But when I get this nervous, nothing is funny.

LUCY: How can I help?

JOHN: I'm not sure. My knees are shaking, palms sweating…like I'm in danger. But there is nothing here, nothing that should cause me to get ready to rumble, to fight, to yell, or to punch somebody's lights out. I just hate it. I hate that I don't have any…(*realization dawning*) any…control.

LUCY: But you do have control.

JOHN: I do? (*He looks around, under the chair.*) Where?

LUCY: You have control because you haven't yelled or punched me out—yet.

JOHN: Well then, don't make me mad.

LUCY: So you want me to do what the bishop wants and walk on eggshells with you?

JOHN (*realization dawning*): Oh no! Oh! That's...that's what Maggie says whenever I get this way. She has to walk on eggshells, like I'm ready to explode.

LUCY: Are you?

JOHN: No, I'm not. Strange...hm-m-m...curious...

LUCY: What's curious?

JOHN: I've gone down a couple of notches. And all we did was talk about it.

LUCY: Well, you know what they say.

JOHN: No, what is that?

LUCY: We are only as sick as our secrets. Maybe you just popped one.

JOHN: Well, it's odd...embarrassing...especially when I can't control it. But it only happens after going to church meetings. Those are the meetings where...where everyone is...is...

LUCY: Out of control?

JOHN: Yes! That's it!

LUCY: What's it?

JOHN: I finally figured it out. I'm allergic!

LUCY: Allergic? Allergic to what?

JOHN: *To church!* I'm allergic to church!

LUCY (*pausing*): And *you* think *my* humor is nuts?

SPEAKER: Thank you all for participating. Take some time to get comfortable.

(*Chairs are moved; noise stops.*)

SPEAKER: Thank you all for your participation. Now take a few minutes for each threesome to debrief the experience of being in your group as the speaker, the listener, and the observer.

MARK: Well, there is no doubt about it. The hardest role for me was the observer role.

JOHN: Me too.

LUCY: Count me in. I wanted to talk.

JOHN: You did talk. You kept joking.

75

Lucy: Until you told me to shut up!

John: Oh, I did. I'm so sorry. I should not have—

Lucy (*interrupting*): Oh yes, you should! How else am I going to get honest feedback? You did well—in fact, too well. And I'm really glad you're here, here with us.

Mark: Me too. But back to being in the observer role. I wanted to rescue something.

Lucy: I wanted to make everyone happy.

John: I wanted to take charge and have order.

MARK, LUCY, and John: (*All give a collective big sigh, then there is silence.*)

Mark: We are…so-o-o sick.

John: So-o-o hopeless.

Lucy: See no evil, hear no evil, speak—

Mark and John (*interrupting*): Lucy!

Lucy: What? It's better than Larry, Curly, and Mo!

Act 2, Scene 1: Return to the Conference Speaker

(*All participants have returned to their seats.*)

Speaker: Thank you again for participating. You need to remember these odd and embarrassing behaviors for future group activities. You will all get an assignment, instead of a lecture, based on your identified odd behavior. You may wish to discuss the assignment with your group or choose to meditate on the assignment just on your own. If, however, you would like to talk with a trauma expert, we have many who came to this conference as volunteers to provide safety nets as you do your trauma work.

Audience Member: What do you mean, "safety nets"?

Speaker: Unless people feel safe enough to talk, nobody would talk. That was painfully obvious with the Fort Hood massacre, where people were shot and killed. Afterward, they had what they called a debriefing. But they didn't make the debriefing safe. They should have organized it in a way that only the people who were directly involved would be present. Instead, everyone came, even those who had nothing to do with the shooting, came to the debriefing. And so nobody talked. It was not safe. There were no safeguards in place to make it safe. And sadly, there were consequences. (*A long pause follows.*)

So, we invited trauma experts today. These people who are trained to handle trauma, in fact, volunteered to be here and to talk to the people present today. With this firsthand experience, we hope to let everyone know that resources exist, and that you don't have to remain stuck in trauma. We organized this conference in a way that everyone would feel safe talking. As you return to your churches, you must keep in mind the importance of making your congregation safe to talk. Debriefings need safeguards. AUDIENCE MEMBER: Thank you.

SPEAKER: You're welcome. There is a schedule where the trauma experts are available. The scheduling times are as follows… (*His voice fades into the background.*)

JOHN (*whispering*): The shrinks are here! There goes the neighborhood!

MARK (*whispering*): I wouldn't mind having a conversation if it might help me get rid of this thing about small spaces, dark places.

JOHN: You would?

MARK: Sure, why not? I've referred many people to counseling. And most got what they needed.

LUCY (*whispering*): I didn't get as much as I needed, but it didn't hurt me, either. So, I'll sign up. I'll go.

SPEAKER: Again, all these times are available to you. And thanks again to all the trauma experts, for your kind generosity in sharing your expertise in this conference. Please help me thank them for their presence. (*Applause sounds.*)

We will continue to follow the PowerPoint presentation. I will make every effort to stick to the agenda as outlined, but there are no guarantees. Getting the trauma conversation going is the whole point of the conference. But sometimes, when dialogue starts, it's hard to stop a body in motion.

We have come from many paths and walks to talk about church trauma, healing church trauma to be specific. However, we need a common language to share and unite us as we walk on our trauma journey together.

Trauma means many things to many people. We experience trauma when we perceive our lives are threatened, or when we are in mortal danger. We experience trauma when our minds are overwhelmed, leaving us swimming in terror, drowning in powerlessness, vulnerability, and loss of control.

When trauma happens, we react in order to survive. With trauma, we do not respond with creativity, logic, or empathy from our wood-chipping processor. Instead, we react with raw survival instinct from the lower part of the brain. We use the survival skills of fight, flight, or freeze. Then, after the trauma is done, we condemn ourselves for being powerless with the words "I shoulda, woulda, or coulda" and "Because I did or didn't, I must be bad, weak, stupid, crazy, lazy, or cowardly." These negative self-talks are our reaction to maintain an illusion of control.

JOHN: Are you saying that self-condemnation is an attempt to maintain control?

SPEAKER: Yes, but control is an illusion. We hang on to the illusion of control even when we have none.

JOHN: But why?

SPEAKER: Which one of you likes being out of control? (*No one raises their hand.*) So, no one likes being out of control. How come?

AUDIENCE MEMBER: Because it triggers danger. We feel...so vulnerable.

JOHN: So, we would rather self-blame than be vulnerable? SPEAKER: Yes.

JOHN: So self-blaming is a natural reaction to trauma?

SPEAKER: Yes. Blame is better than the powerlessness and loss of control that we experience from trauma.

JOHN: And so you're saying we self-blame to pretend we coulda-shoulda-woulda had control, if only we had...had...

SPEAKER: Had done something different than what we did?

JOHN: Yes.

SPEAKER: So, "If only I had run faster, left the house earlier, went straight instead of turning, avoided that store, things would have been different. I coulda, shoulda, woulda had control and avoided the trauma." Does this make any sense?

JOHN: Well, kinda…

SPEAKER (*pausing*): Let me use a personal example. When my spouse was dying of cancer, I woulda-coulda-shoulded myself into a self-eviscerating assessment: "If you were any kind of a decent partner, you would've helped, protected, or cured your loved one. You should've controlled the outcome."

It all felt so true. But it only *felt* true because the trauma of the disease had overloaded my mind with pictures of suffering. Images jammed the creative-logical-empathetic processor of my brain and went right into memory storage. These pictures were raw, graphic, and powerful enough to knock me down and bring me to my knees.

If that trauma had been left un-debriefed, if I had not received post-trauma care, had I not processed, integrated, and learned from that prolonged horrible event, I would still be self-eviscerating until now. I would still be woulda-coulda-shoulda-ing myself, still reacting with the instinctual survival skills of fight, flight, and freeze whenever triggered. Without the intervention that I received, those intrusive pictures—powerful enough to cause post- trauma reactions—would continue to knock me down until I, too, enter the grave.

LUCY: But why would you do that to yourself? (*Audience reacts with stillness.*)

MARK (*whispering*): Careful, Lucy.

LUCY: You didn't cause it, couldn't control it, and couldn't cure it. So, why did you do it?

SPEAKER: I said that over and over: "I didn't cause this, can't control it, can't cure it." My mind accepted them, but my heart would never listen and my body paid any attention to what my head was saying. Each time a song was played, a familiar phrase was spoken…her picture was seen, or even certain smells …I could not help but react. My body reacted. Sometimes, it reacted was nausea. Sometimes, my knees just buckled and I went to the floor. Sometimes, I couldn't breathe. But whatever happened, it was not something I would choose for myself or even my worst enemy. It was just…just there—and sometimes still is.

Lucy: But that…that is so…painful. Can't you just…just let it go?

Speaker: I don't have the option to let it go.

Lucy: What do you mean?

Speaker: I don't have the option just to let it go. My choices are face the pain and disempower the images, or, be post- trauma haunted the rest of my life. I chose to face the pain and disempower the images. And, in order to do that, I had to help my body heal from living in the post trauma land of fight, flight, and freeze.

Lucy: So, what did you gain by facing the pain?

Speaker: I got more pain.

Lucy: More pain?

Speaker: Yes. The pain of grieving. I could not begin to process grief pain until I stopped reacting to the mental videos of the daily death march, which took my spouse down, piece by piece, knowing there was nothing I could do, to stop it. My body had to calm down from those traumatic memories through deep belly breathing, thoracic muscle relaxation, body awareness, and bilateral movement. Once I learned how to calm my body through those intentional body interventions, I was able to process the intrusive images and triggers, and learn about me. And I learned that when my body was calm, my thinking returned. I was able to identify both my thoughts and feelings, and learn from them. With a calm body, I learned that I could use my mind to know what was true and what wasn't. And with a calm body, I could choose not to believe the lies of self eviscerations. And so, when I learned how to manage my body's post trauma reaction with body solutions, I could swim in deep waters, and learn about me, and the depth of my grief. And what I learned about my grief, was that it was only a mere reflection of the depth of my love for my spouse. My calmed body no longer blocked me from that knowledge. And knowing in the depths of my mind, my heart, and my body that the terrible pain of grief was really a reflection of the depths of my love, I could then begin my grief journey.

LUCY: You are still there, on the journey. SPEAKER: (pause) Yes... You noticed.

LUCY: Yeah.

SPEAKER: The grief of a beloved spouse never goes away. You just learn to be...to be more honest.

LUCY (*tearing up, voice starting to crack*): Thank you. Thank you very much.

SPEAKER: You're welcome, Lucy. Now...more questions? (*The audience fades out.*)

MARK: Lucy, are you okay?

LUCY: Yeah. That was more truth than what I'm used to. But it's odd.

MARK: What's odd?

LUCY: I feel...feel safer now, more than I've ever felt.

JOHN: Me too. Like the boogeyman left the building.

MARK: Or we're just breaking the rules.

JOHN: The rules?

MARK: The happy, happy-face church rules.

LUCY: Those rules aren't here. This...this is real.

MARK AND JOHN: What?

LUCY: It's real. I feel safe because of the honesty, because *we* are all for real.

SPEAKER: Again, good questions. Okay, what about churches? How do churches do trauma?

Many churches are stuck in post-trauma reaction, haunted by forgotten, unprocessed trauma memory.

To the untrained eye, the people just appear to be just plain nutty, cranky, controlling, rude, and dismissive. They appear to be numb to their own feelings, as well as numb to the feelings of others. But those are trauma's footprints—

81

people reacting with fight, flight, or freeze. These survival reactions are triggered by as simple as words, thoughts, or images. They can also be triggered by discussions, sights, sounds, voice tones, unfamiliar situations, changes, or even new ideas.

AUDIENCE MEMBER 1: What do you mean, "New ideas"? How can new ideas trigger survival reactions?

SPEAKER: Good question. What typically is said when new ideas are introduced in church? Anyone?

LUCY: *We've never done it that way before!*

SPEAKER: Yes! Has anyone *not* heard that reaction to newly introduced ideas? (*He pauses.*) So, you have all heard that reaction, the reaction of how ideas are shot down. But how does that happen? Where do those words come from? When did the church start saying it? What were the circumstances when they began saying it? And why is it unchallenged?

LUCY: That church is DOA!

SPEAKER: Yes, Lucy, dead on arrival. All because no one has asked the questions and looked at the history of the church. Could "we never did it that way before" also be a survival reaction, a post-trauma survival reaction where people are in survival mode? Are they cranky, controlling, and numb? But no one ever knows because the questions are never asked.

LUCY (*whispered singing*): And the beat goes on!

SPEAKER: So why make a big deal out of church trauma? There is no blood. There are no limbs on the floor and no smell of burning flesh. What makes church trauma a big deal? (*He waits.*)

MARK: The stakes are higher.

SPEAKER: Hm-m-m. How are they higher?

MARK: They are higher because the terror of losing one's life is not the same as the terror of losing one's *eternal* life.

SPEAKER: Hm-m-m, so those entrusted with the words of eternal life have a unique responsibility.

MARK: Yeah. Responsibility *not* to use them to skewer the sheep!

SPEAKER: And what happens when they are used to skewer the sheep?

LUCY: Lamb chops! (*The audience laughs.*) Serving lamb chops, fresh and hot lamb chops.

SPEAKER: Lucy, we're taking it on the road! (*He waits for the audience.*) But how does leadership abuse the sheep?

AUDIENCE MEMBER: You're going to hell if you don't *do* what I tell you.

SECOND AUDIENCE MEMBER: Or *say* what I tell you.

THIRD AUDIENCE MEMBER: Or *believe* what I tell you!

SPEAKER: Now what do you call it when the words of eternal life are used to tell people don't think, don't feel, or don't move?

AUDIENCE MEMBER: Prison!

ANOTHER AUDIENCE MEMBER: Dysfunctional family!

THIRD AUDIENCE MEMBER: A cult!

LUCY: *Hold the Kool-Aid!* (*The audience nervously chuckles.*)

SPEAKER: Very descriptive. There are several ways to wound the sheep, to beat them, to traumatize them with the words of eternal life. But usually, the church is traumatized by leadership in the following four ways (*He uses the PowerPoint.*):

Using doctrine or the Bible to violate conscience, silence opposition, or to dismiss health concerns.

Using doctrine or the Bible to build one's own kingdom of power and take control over others through ideology, political deception, and intrigue.

Using people to advance one's career and grandiose dreams of entitlement.

Using people to fulfill one's own sensual wants and desires.

MARK: But don't you think doctrine is important?

SPEAKER: Doctrine is important. But what is more important is *how* doctrine is used.

MARK: How it's used? What do you mean? Doctrine is doctrine.

SPEAKER: And what is the purpose of doctrine?

LUCY: Doctrine reflects the true nature of God—that God is loving, forgiving, and gracious. (*She pauses; then there is applause from the audience.*)

SPEAKER: Thank you. Lucy the wolverine now-turned teddy bear! (*All chuckle.*) But is that enough?

LUCY: Enough what? What else is there? God is loving, forgiving, and gracious.

SPEAKER: The "what else" that's missing is the context.

LUCY: The context? What context?

SPEAKER: The context is trauma. The missing context from "God is loving, forgiving, and gracious" is the trauma. Is there a trauma conversation? That God is loving— *through the trauma of the cross*? And forgiving and gracious—*through the trauma of the cross*?

LUCY: But isn't that…that…just assumed?

SPEAKER: Assumed by whom?

LUCY: Well, by…by…by me, I guess.

SPEAKER: So why assume that the trauma conversation automatically happens when you speak about God's love, grace, and forgiveness?

LUCY: No (*realization dawning*)…no, it doesn't happen. It does need the context. It needs the trauma conversation. Because it's always in the context of the Traumatized One!SPEAKER: And what happens when a church goes without the trauma context?

JOHN: You end up with people wearing masks.

SPEAKER: What kind of masks?

JOHN: The plastic, smiley-faced Jesus masks! (*A few amens sound from the audience.*)

SPEAKER: Is that safe?

JOHN: No, it's not safe. Not safe for traumatized people, not safe or healthy for anyone *not* wearing a plastic smiley face.

SPEAKER: So, it's not safe or healthy to be in a church of the plastic smiley face. The place is not for people struggling with trauma.

AUDIENCE MEMBER: Why not? SPEAKER: Any takers?

MARK: If I'm traumatized, eventually I won't be welcomed without my smiley face. I'll be the nail that sticks out, like the only sober member of an alcoholic family.

SPEAKER: Ouch! An unpleasant thought.

Now none of you has to answer this right now, but think, how many of you can say with absolute certainty that your church *does not have* plastic smiley-face doctrines? (*He looks at the audience; dead silence.*) Okay, we'll let that cook some more.

So, the purpose of doctrine is to reflect God's true nature—that God is loving, forgiving, and gracious, *in the context of trauma* – both God's and our own. Now what if that doctrine is used for some other purpose? Let's say it's used to tell people to shut up or gain control over others or deceive or fulfill their own dreams and desires. Is it still doctrine? Or has it become…something else?

AUDIENCE MEMBER: I don't understand the question. What could it become other than what it is?

SPEAKER: Good question. A surgeon's scalpel was made for doing good. It is an instrument of healing; that is its purpose. However, what do you call a scalpel used to murder someone?

AUDIENCE MEMBER: A murder weapon?

SPEAKER: Yes. It stopped being what it was and became something else.

JOHN: So your point is that doctrine, when used to do good by being loving, forgiving, and gracious, is doctrine. And that's true, until someone uses it against its purpose?

SPEAKER: Thank you. Now when patience, honesty, and humor are present, there is much room in the church for conversation. It encourages discussion and disagreement over doctrine, over the interpretations of the words of eternal life.

However, two Bible passages are quite clear. These two passages tell us how we should treat each other, even at times of disagreements. They are found throughout the Bible. Join with me and say: "You shall *love* the Lord your God (*The audience joins in.*)…with all your heart, all your soul, and all your mind; and you shall *love* your neighbor as yourself." Thank you. These are the love doctrines. So how do these doctrines work in the church?

MARK: The love doctrines are trump cards.

SPEAKER: Trump cards?

MARK: Yeah. Love trumps all doctrinal or interpretative disagreements. If other doctrines trump love, then it's already "sheep, now being served in the dining room." (*The audience laughs.*)

SPEAKER: You're sitting with a Badger and a Wolverine; which one are you?

MARK: Neither. I'm a Buckeye!

SPEAKER: The apocalypse has come! (*The audience laughs.*) Badgers and buckeyes and wolverines—oh my!

MARK: Thou preparest a table before me, in the presence of my. . . (*The audience laughs.*)

SPEAKER (*waiting for audience*): That's quite a table. And your name?

MARK: I'm Mark, and thank *you* for being here, and for your leadership.

SPEAKER: You're welcome. Now questions about love trumping all disagreements. Questions?

AUDIENCE MEMBER: My question is this. Aren't we supposed to take sides based on our beliefs?

LUCY (*jumping in*): Sure! But when things get screwed up, always, always err on the side of love, forgiveness, and grace. (*The audience applauds.*)

SPEAKER: Lucy from Michigan, I'm taking you with me!

LUCY: (*holding out her left hand, flashing her diamond wedding ring*): Too late. I'm already taken—by another Wolverine! (*The audience laughs.*)

SPEAKER: Ya snooze, ya lose! (*He waits for the audience laughter to quiet.*) Now there is another passage of Scripture that describes the job of church leadership. It is very clear. It has not changed ever since. Anyone remember this job description? It's only a one-liner. Anyone want to give this a shot?

JOHN: I'll give it a shot. "The Good Shepherd lays down His life for the sheep."

SPEAKER: Yes. Now, look real close. Does it say the Good Shepherd lays down His life for a doctrine?

AUDIENCE: No!

SPEAKER: How about, for an interpretation of the Scripture?

AUDIENCE: No!

SPEAKER: Or even, for an ideology or political agenda? AUDIENCE: No!

SPEAKER: What about, for whatever I can get over, get away with, or get *from* the sheep?

AUDIENCE: No! No! No!

SPEAKER: So, the Good Shepherd...lays His life down...for the sheep. The sheep are not there for the shepherd's own gratification. Three times Jesus told Peter, "*Feed* My sheep", *not* "Fleece My sheep"! (*There are a few amens from the audience.*)

MARK: But how do we nourish the sheep when the sheep have been beaten—beaten and traumatized? In fact, how do we even recognize the sheep's post-trauma reactions?

SPEAKER: Good questions. By the end of this conference, you will be able to answer them by recognizing post-trauma reaction—in yourselves. (*He pauses.*)

We are coming up on a long break. During the break, your group assignment is to think of your odd experiences in your church. Then, look at the history of your church, but this time, you must view your church's history through the lens of trauma.

And then ask yourselves these questions: Are there unexplained, odd reactions during church discussions? When did you start noticing them? Have there ever been abuses of power in your congregation? And how did the church deal with that trauma?

Have a good break, but be back in an hour. (*John bolts out of his chair and leaves.*)

MARK: John! Where you going?

JOHN (*not looking back*): Out!

MARK: John?

JOHN (*speaking over his shoulder*): I need some air!

MARK AND LUCY (*looking at each other and speaking simultaneously*): Let's roll!

(*They rush out to find John.*)

Discussion Questions
(Act 1, Scene 4)

Part 1

1. John gave a gift to both his pastors, a church sign reading, "Enter at own Risk: Park your hearts and brains at the door." Was this meant to be humorous? Why or why not? Have you experienced being treated oddly after sharing a feeling or a personal thought or idea in church? Is your church safe for people to share their hurts and sorrows? What policies, places, and organizational structures exist to help people feel safe when they speak their hearts and minds?

2. What do you think of the expectation that the church should only be a happy place? Is your church a place of healing, or is it more concerned about being seen as happy? Have you ever shared your hurts, sorrows, and trauma with church people? Have you ever heard anyone share their negative experiences of life in the church?

3. Just thinking about being the speaker in the group caused John to go into a fight reaction. How do you think Lucy helped him to de-escalate his reaction? What would you do?

Possible Responses to DQ

1. It was probably meant to be a joke. Still, it shouldn't be because it enables burying emotions as a response to trauma. Everyone goes through an experience of being treated differently after sharing something personal, but the reaction to this depends on the person who shared, whether they move on from the incident or hide their emotions instead, which is a much more likely scenario. Freedom of expression is something that is recognized and practiced greatly

in plenty of churches. It should be something that is exercised as a common rule.

2. These rules can either help make a church a happier and safer place, but most churches today implement rules that repress their people from true healing. It is a normal human action to share experiences, but sometimes, people refrain in constant or occasional fear of being judged or being treated differently.

3. As John was slightly moving into a state of fight, something similar to panic, Lucy began to ease him down with an attempt to cool or calm him through humor and nonsense—which ultimately worked.

Discussion Questions
(Act 1, Scene 4)

Part 2

1. When Lucy shared her "odd behavior" of fast eating, she used much humor. How do you think she did using her humor? Did it help or defocus her from sharing? What advice would be tempting to give to Lucy, and would it work, if this was her survival reaction to trauma?

2. Mark shared his feeling of being trapped whenever he is in small and dark places. What do you think of his avoidance of small, dark places? What makes you feel trapped?

3. What made the 3 of them begin to share their odd behaviors with each other? How do you think they were able to talk about something so painful? Would you consider going to a trauma expert for healing?

Possible Responses to DQ

1. Lucy herself realized that she uses her humor as a way to deflect the problems she is facing at hand. She is aware and recognizes that one of her defense mechanisms is humor, yet she doesn't have a clear understanding as to why that is. Probably the best advice to give her, in this case, is to say that it isn't exactly a bad thing to joke around. However, when it comes to facing her problems, it might be better to be serious yet still maintain a slightly lighthearted attitude. It would balance her defense coping mechanism with her desire to find the solution to her problem. How would you help her find the balance? What if humor was her post trauma reaction?

2. It's a form of escapism, the way he continues to avoid small spaces rather than get used to the idea of them, which is not a very good solution for him in the long run. Personally, I think that unanswered questions make me feel trapped more than anything. And what if John's reaction to small spaces, dark places was a post trauma reaction? How would you help him?

3. It started off as quite a joke for them, with some hesitance in the air, but not long enough, they started to face what they thought each other knew already. It made them mention these things easier because they thought it was information the other two already noticed, when in fact, they haven't. Trauma experts are experts for a reason, and it definitely would help, if not a lot, then even at least a little, with the healing process.

Discussion Questions
(Act 2, Scene 1)

1. Is your congregation safe enough to talk about trauma? What makes a congregation safe? What steps would you take to make your congregation safe? What is the cost of an unsafe church? What effect does the lack of safety have on the mission, outreach, and compassion?

2. In the face of powerlessness, we tend to blame and condemn ourselves rather than embrace our powerlessness. Do you use the words "woulda - coulda - shoulda" in talking about yourself? Where does saying that to yourself get you? Is it helpful or hurtful? Wouldn't it be better just to bury the trauma and be done with it?

3. If a doctrine or the Bible is used to manipulate, control, or take from the people of God, is it still doctrine? Is it following the purpose of the church, to raise the dead, comfort the afflicted, and heal the sick? If the primary doctrine of the church is that all need to wear a plastic smiley face while in church, how do we treat the traumatized, and what will be said to them to get them to bury the trauma? How does The Cross fit into the trauma conversation?

Possible Responses to DQ

1. The church is supposed to be a community where you feel united with the people you are with. Feeling unsafe in this type of environment would defeat the purpose and intention that God has for these congregations. Compassion cannot exist in a community without empathy, and without empathy, there is no understanding and bridge for connection with each other.

2. The "woulda-coulda-shoulda" phrases are what mostly lead people into feeling worse than they should. It makes them overthink and feel smaller than they are. It's quite hurtful

because you get swallowed by the negative thoughts and feel like you will never be able to move on and feel positive again. Buried trauma rots, creating a bad smell that sticks to your mind. What do people get out of using the "woulda-coulda-shouldas"? What is it that is being avoided?

3. The doctrine becomes another thing, like how a scalpel can become a murder weapon. Humans have the power to think, as we are the only rational beings made by God, and we were given a choice to do good or to do the opposite. God accepts everyone - from beggars to sinners who repent, to the ill. We should not hide our trauma, faults, and negativity just to act like we are okay. Jesus himself has openly shown us that we are accepted no matter what, as long as we have faith and we believe in the Church.

CHAPTER 5:

The Rubber Hits the Road

What do you think of a teacher that doesn't teach? Or a doctor that does not treat? Are they doing a disservice to their profession? How about in the church? Have you ever attended a church that does not promote God's teaching and healing? Have you ever known a church leader who disguises his own motives using the name of God and the Bible? If so, what has been your reaction to such churches and leaders?

Commentary

There are no classes taught in seminary to understand the dynamics of trauma—how it affects individuals and how traumatizing leadership impacts organizations. Based on a first responder study, spirituality is the best predictor of post-trauma growth, yet not a single book talks about the theology of trauma, it's healing and teaching. Consequently, blindness and ignorance keep the trauma cycle going, on and on through the post-trauma reaction. As old Yogi Berra, the baseball player, once remarked, "It's déjà vu, all over again!"

The trauma conversation was abandoned by the church centuries ago. The church kept the cross—the trauma's symbol—but the trauma conversation was lost. It was replaced with forms of conversations that only extolled the virtues of centralized power and control. Faith became measurable in ways such as one's belief on the doctrine and by the successful accumulation of worldly goods. After all, the evidence of God's blessing has to be our successes, our triumphs, and our ability to make people do, believe, and give to us whatever we tell them. Paradoxically, the church did the opposite of its symbol and became just one more-worldly traumatizer on a landscape littered by a plethora of them.

In abandoning the conversation, the church produced traumatizing leadership styles focused on accumulating more power and control. Church leaders became experts at using doctrine, the Bible, and church people for their own pursuit of power. And almost instinctively, they justify such horrible acts with "I'm doing this for God!"

Therefore, this kind of shepherd definitely does not care for the sheep. Instead, it encourages the sheep to be slaughtered, abused, burned and tortured for simply daring to disagree and speak their conscience. In other words, the sheep were traumatized by the shepherds themselves! Instead of the church being a sanctuary—a safe place offering hospitality for the weary—it becomes a horror house, especially for the bold people who dare not comply with the church's agenda.

Sad enough, the church became a traumatizing agent itself after it abandoned the trauma conversation. Nonetheless, some courageous people saw this problem and decided to act accordingly. The earlier attempts include the monastic movements, the Reformation movement, and the theology of the cross movements. Later on, a theology of suffering was offered by its first eloquent martyr, Dietrich Bonhoeffer. It is followed by the renowned Martin Luther King, Jr. However, these corrective actions were unsustainable because they never directly addressed trauma. To have a long-lasting effect, what needs to be directly addressed is this:

1. What do we do with trauma in ourselves and others, and
2. Does God have anything to say about our trauma?

The good news is that God has much to say about trauma. First, God himself suffered and became the Traumatized One. Thereafter, he said, "Follow Me." In other words, God's will is expressed in the second commandment, *Don't use the Lord's name in vain.* It simply means that one must not use God's name to traumatize others. God's will is for us to be faithful in our relationships, not to become successful nor to prove that we are always right. God invites us with his words, "Follow Me and heal the sick, raise the dead, comfort the afflicted." Following God means to become experts in caring for the world's traumatized, not become the cause of it.

The second piece of good news is this. God became the Traumatized One so that all of us who have experienced trauma might have the conversation with the one eternal friend who intimately understands us and our trauma. Within the dialogue, we might experience the love, grace, and forgiveness of an open-hearted God.

The bad news is that this good news remains missing in most church curricula, training, gatherings, and worship experiences. Therefore, not only is the church susceptible to trauma, but it can also, be a major supplier of it. But the church cannot even learn from trauma because there are no words to even talk about it.

Accordingly, traumatizing cycles can go on for as long as four hundred years! Without the conversation, the church has neither prevention strategies, healing plans, nor therapeutic responses to trauma. The church condems itself to blind, unending post-trauma reaction instead of post-trauma growth. To paraphrase a popular movie, "Either the church needs to get busy healing or get busy burying," because, without the good news of the God who transforms trauma, there is no in-between.

The church has been called to occupy a special place in human life. These roles are to follow Jesus and enter the world with healing. But not is the case anymore. Is the church's decreasing relevance a result of our unwillingness to keep this very core responsibility? Are we not called to lift the cross up high?

Reader's Theatre

Act 2, Scene 2: The Conference Parking lot

Mark and Lucy go out the side door and find John. As they go toward him, John is pacing.

JOHN (*demanding, ready to blow*): Why weren't we told all of these before?

MARK: Told what?

JOHN (*yelling*): About trauma. Before...before...twelve years ago!

MARK: They didn't know.

JOHN: Oh, bull! The bishop knew!

MARK: He couldn't have known. Army chaplains maybe, but not the rest of—

JOHN (*interrupting, screaming*): Shut up! Just shut up! Shut up!

MARK (*after a long pause*): Did you say that...to them?

JOHN (*sobbing*): No, no! No, I didn't. I didn't say it to either the pastor, that expert, or the bishop. I-I tried to...but, I couldn't talk...couldn't think...

MARK: Couldn't say anything.

JOHN: He put gag orders on the staff...made them sign loyalty oaths...and I couldn't stop him!

MARK: A Gestapo...

JOHN: And he closed all the meetings in order to avoid any Questions. Then he and his sycophants went into "executive session" to cover his tracks. He humiliated us, threatened us, blamed us. He used the Scripture and told us that we would be compromising the Word of God whenever we disagree with him. That we had jeopardized our eternal salvation if we didn't go along with him. That we weren't true to the confessions, the doctrines. We weren't true believers if...if we did not...did not...

MARK: Did not park your brains and hearts at the church door?

JOHN: Oh my God! (*He immediately stops sobbing.*) The sign—*my* sign! I've worn that sign. For twelve years, I've carried that sign!

LUCY: But that's not all you're carrying, is it, John?

JOHN: No, no it isn't. When it became clear he would not get his own way…that there were too many of us taking our brains *inside* the church…he tried to take out the whole church. He tried to just kill us off. He didn't succeed. But he turned us against each other and divided the church. And when he left, he took people with him, people who had been my friends since childhood. My friends—and we haven't spoken since.

LUCY: But that wasn't the worst of it, was it, John?

JOHN: No, it wasn't. After he left, people figured him out. Eventually most saw his game—his schtick, his con. And so they left the faith. They were disillusioned, they blamed God, and now they go nowhere. They are nowhere. They are just lost…lost sheep without a shepherd.

LUCY (*after a moment's silence*): John, this is really painful.

JOHN (*pauses, takes a deep breath, and whispers*): Yeah. I'm sorry, so sorry. I shouldn't have yelled at you. I just…just…

MARK: Just keep on breathing, ol' buddy. Deep breathing… You're doing fine… We're not going anywhere.

LUCY: We love you, John. And maybe it wouldn't be a bad idea to sign up to have a conversation with one of the trauma experts. It wouldn't hurt. After all, how could you get any more miserable than you already are?

JOHN: Don't make me laugh, Lucy.

LUCY: And if you don't get what you need, then maybe they'll refund all your misery!

JOHN: Lucy, you're such an idiot!

LUCY: But I'm a darling idiot. And you love me, don't you? (*John smiles.*)

LUCY: I saw that! I saw that! John, you're smiling. Caught you smiling! You do love me. Go ahead and say it.

MARK: Lucy!

LUCY: C'mon, John. I know you want to. Say it!

JOHN (*still smiling*): I don't want to say it.

LUCY: Oh yes, you do! You want to say it. C'mon, John, say it! C'mon.

JOHN (*still smiling*): All right, okay, I'll say it. *I love Lucy!*

LUCY: Yes! (*She does a victory dance, arms in the air.*) Now don't you feel better?

JOHN (*pausing*): Yeah. But you're still an idiot—a lovable idiot!

MARK: So tell us, what happened in there? What triggered you?

JOHN: I was okay 'til he got to the part describing the four kinds of leadership abuse. It was in that very moment, I pictured his smiling...his self-righteous...plastic...grin again.

MARK: That's a picture! I wouldn't want it in my head. So he actually abused the church with *all four types* of leadership abuse?

JOHN: Well, put it this way: he clearly got three out of four. MARK AND LUCY (*looking at each other*): Batting 750!

JOHN: And he did it with that...that plastic grin. He grinned while he barefaced lied to me. All the time! He kept telling everyone how wonderful he was. He was dividing up the church's assets. And even us. But in his spare time, he was running for a higher church office.

LUCY: A higher church office? You mean, he wanted a bigger church?

JOHN: Nope, higher.

MARK: He was campaigning to be a bishop?

JOHN: Nope, higher than that.

MARK: Well, what's higher than being a bishop?

JOHN: He was out campaigning to sit at the left hand of God (*He starts laughing.*)...because...because...

LUCY AND MARK: Because the right hand was already taken! (*All three are laughing now.*)

JOHN: You got it! But thank God his conspiracy of lies unraveled. He just ran out of people to blame. But it's still hard to believe, that after all these years, that people actually followed him, that they were so...so...

LUCY: So vulnerable?

JOHN: Yes.

LUCY: And so open to be led—led and used?

JOHN: Yes.

MARK: Well, that's why we're called sheep.

JOHN: He certainly cooked some mutton on the "barbe."

LUCY: Now there you go! Got some humor back, do we?

MARK: I hate to break up this festival, but we need to get back in there.

LUCY: I'm game. John, you ready for another leg of lamb?

JOHN: I might as well go back for seconds. Pandora's Box is open. There's no turning back now. (*He walks toward the entrance and then stops.*) No retreat! No surrender! (*He goes inside.*)

Discussion Questions

1. What do you make out of John's strong reaction after hearing the 4 ways leadership traumatizes congregations? Are his wounds still a problem? If they are, when and where do they become problematic? If you had been used, manipulated, and lied to in the church, would you still go? Has that ever happened to you? How did you heal from that experience?

2. What happens to the church family when leadership uses its authority to put self first and divide the sheep? What happens to the creative, logical, empathetic discussion when leadership encourages people to "Park your brains and hearts at the door?" Does God want us to serve Him without hearts and brains?

3. John begins to connect the dots regarding his seemingly uncontrollable anger and his church experience twelve years ago. What do you think was underneath his anger? Would you have the same strong reactions about what was done to the church? Why or why not? How do you think Mark and Lucy helped John during his anger?

Possible Responses to DQ

1. John's realizations on how he had gained trauma without realizing it and acting the way he did was a valid reaction. A person's wounds don't heal by themselves unless the wound is really shallow. However, John had more than one deep wound. It became problematic when he didn't realize it until then, but it was understandable. After all, he hadn't known he was being manipulated because he was terrified, controlled, and filled with fear. Manipulation, which is a form of betrayal, takes our fears and heightens them, which is why we choose to forget rather than face them.

2. The church becomes less than a church. It loses its meaning. And when people are told to leave both hearts and minds out of the picture, this creates zombies—or in the context of the church, mindless sheep. God always wants us to be compassionate and rational, which is why it is never the right decision to leave these two behind.

3. Behind this anger was clearly pain and fear. He was subjected to manipulation that went so far. The congregation was divided and, in a way, murdered. Understandably, this sparked many negative emotions in John. He ultimately felt alone after the experience, and the presence of Mark and Lucy being there and trying to help him smile through it aided the process of recovering from his post-traumatic anger that was triggered by the discussion.

CHAPTER 6:

Three Stories

*If you are given a chance to look at the past, what would be the
first things that you'd look into? Would you use such a chance to
look for answers? Would you be brave enough to search for historical
explanations of the present to change your life and circumstances
for the better? Or would you rather be enslaved and jailed by
an unknown past that has been haunting you for long?*

Commentary

John is clearly embarrassed about his instinctive reaction and attitude that were witnessed by his pastors. Nevertheless, John screaming "Shut up!" is quite understandable because his traumatizer did
shut him up, too.

Stored in his mental toxic waste site, the un-debriefed, unprocessed, and un-integrated images of the church sign and the plastic
pastor smile can still easily be triggered from the past into the present. Thus, it can be concluded that his "shut up!" fight survival reaction was never meant for that place and time. Instead, it was meant
for his past. His buried memory was triggered even by the smallest
information regarding church trauma. And it didn't take much for
that small information to turn John into his cranky self.

The mental pictures of the church twelve years ago are still so powerful because they remain un-debriefed. They were unprocessed because the questions had not been pursued, understood, or answered. There was no language framework to make sense out of the experience. Lastly, the pictures were non-integrated into his awareness because, as you may remember, he had even joked about the same sign, unaware that the sign had come from his own buried memory of the traumatic event.

John's church trauma of twelve years ago is still disconnected from his awareness. As such, its impact on his present relationship with God and others remain largely unknown to him. He is simply unaware of his reactions, more so that his reactions are tied to trauma.

The intrigue, the deception, and the misuse of God's name still color his mood. The memories of the misconducts and betrayal of a person of the cloth still outrage John, keeping others at a distance, and crippling his spirituality. Twelve years later, the trauma is still not over. Time does not heal all wounds, but time does bury the trauma deeper and deeper, disconnecting it from John's present-day post trauma reactions.

Today, however, there is good news for John. Today he received some clarity and awareness. He clearly saw the trauma and is now aware that it has affected him. In other words, he is now out of denial. It's too late for John to shove the genie back into the bottle or to put a lid on Pandora's Box. He has connected the dots and can no longer step around the elephant in his own life, showing a bliss of blindness. He now has clarity and needs to do something about his newfound awareness. Doing nothing is no longer an option. He's simply too painfully aware of the elephant sitting on his heart. In order to have some peace of mind, he needs to make sense and meaning out of his experience.

During the discussion with Mark and Lucy, John began to connect the dots and decided to go back into the conference and learn a language framework that would help him understand the trauma. His newfound awareness gives him a choice to remain in misery or to finally change and grow.

The formula for traumatizing the sheep has always existed. It persists because it works. This formula consists of the three overused accusations:

"You have compromised the Word of God."
"You are not true to the doctrines [confessions] of the church."
"You have jeopardized your eternal salvation."

Such formula is followed by the doxology, "We must obey God rather than man." But, could this formula and doxology also have arisen from a history of trauma?

Reader's Theatre

Act 2, Scene 3: Back at the Conference

SPEAKER: Thank you all for coming back on time. I am grateful that we have not lost anyone—yet! You are all brave to stay.

The following three stories are church-trauma stories. You have read about the first story in the marketing material for this conference. It is the story of the Protestant church where all the church members used to bow to the blank wall. Some of you are nodding; some of you aren't. Hm-m-m-m, Let me give a brief review.

For four hundred years, generations of people bowed to the church's blank wall. Whenever they enter for worship, they bow without question. Every person who wanted to be a member had to bow as well. Similarly, when children went through training, they were automatically taught to do the same practice.

So out of curiosity, people began asking, "Why does this church bow to the blank wall?" However, such question is greeted with defensive statements such as, "Because that is simply who we are." But in reality, no one had the foggiest idea of how they got stuck bowing to that blank wall.

And then one day, the church had to make some renovations. These renovations involved going into the blank wall. And so they started to work on the blank wall, and to their amazement, they found a beautiful icon of Mary under four inches of plaster behind the wall.

They then explored and found out the truth—their own truth, their true identity. The truth that had been covered over for years was that they really were Catholics. However, four hundred years before, a Protestant prince had violated them, forcing them to become Protestant and taking all of the signs of their true faith away. The prince then plastered over anything that could not be removed. And they were forbidden to speak about their forced conversion, under penalty of death.

But despite this traumatic experience, with their last ounce of courage and strength, these Catholics continued to silently confess their faith. They did that by bowing to the wall where the beautiful image of Mary was plastered. For them, it was a sign of self-definition. It showed who they really were and became their identity in the face of trauma.

But since they were forbidden to speak, their story was eventually forgotten over the years. The strength that kept them bowing to the blank wall was lost. They had no words to tell their story of strength, identity, and survival. There was no conversation to tell the story. Instead, what was left was this very odd, very strange reaction. It was an embarrassment, a source of humiliation that no one could explain.

And so, since the trauma conversation did not happen, the trauma was left unprocessed, separated, and un-integrated from their awareness. Their survival skill continued as a post-trauma reaction. And it would have continued on and on and on if they had not discovered the truth.

My hope is that you walk away from this conference with some truth. And the first truth is that *we all bow to blank walls*. We all do odd, strange, and weird things, things with no apparent causes.

So your first assignment in the previous session was for you to identify your own blank-wall-bowing practices. Now, could that odd behavior be a post trauma reaction, like your own form of bowing to the blank wall?

My hope is that you use the same courage that it took for you to get to this conference to explore your blank walls. I hope that through this conference, you finally find the truth about yourself.

Use your courage and curiosity. Ask the tougher, deeper questions. And then, breathe it in. Breathe what is behind it. Get curious, and the truth will find you—your own truth, God's truth, your neighbor's truth. And then the truth about healing trauma will eventually follow. With this truth, you will become an agent of grace, love, and forgiveness to yourself, to others, and to the church. We can promise that with the proper words and conversation, all trauma will be redeemed and raised to become your lesson and teacher. So, are there any questions or comments?

AUDIENCE MEMBER: But how did you know that bowing to the wall was a post-trauma reaction? (*Voice fades into the background.*)

SPEAKER: We simply asked two questions: When did the odd behavior started to appear, and what was going on during that time? (*Voice fades into the background.*)... Then continue to explore...

JOHN (*whispering*): When you told me that...that blank-wall story, I thought you two were pulling my leg. You mean, that really happened? People bowed to a blank wall for four hundred years?

MARK: It's hard to believe, until you think about our own wall-bowing.

LUCY: That's why he made the assignment. He asked us to take a look at our own odd stuff, the weird stuff we do...like eating fast—greased-lightning fast.

MARK: Or getting strange about small spaces and dark places.

JOHN: Or even screaming at people to shut up.

MARK (*pausing*): Well, I have a bad feeling about this. Maybe we should pack up and leave?

JOHN: Oh no, we're not! The genie's out. We're going ahead—and finding our truth together.

LUCY: It can't be fatal. After all, we might all have weird behavior, but we all survived. It's almost like a symbol, a symbol of life.

MARK: Yeah, yeah, I know. But I don't want it closing in on me.

LUCY: Is it closing in now?

MARK: Yeah.

LUCY: How can we help?

MARK: Do something stupid.

LUCY (*singing quietly*): How much is that doggie in the window? Arf, arf! (*John joins in and sings.*) The one with the wag-ga-ly tail—

MARK (*interrupting*): Sh-h-h! Okay, okay. A little distraction goes a long way.

LUCY: Mark, you are not alone. We're all here—together.

> (*She makes a fist and puts it between the two of them.*) Remember? All for one…

JOHN AND MARK: (*John puts fist out immediately, with Mark reluctantly following.*)

> And one for all.

LUCY: Sh-h-h! He's going to start.

SPEAKER: Thank you for all your questions—very good questions.

> You'll have more. Before the next stories, I'll introduce four key phrases that you may recognize. These phrases are:

> "You have compromised the Word of God."

> "You are unfaithful to the confessions, the church doctrines."

> "You have jeopardized your own salvation." and

> "We must obey God rather than man."

> Anyone ever heard of these phrases?

LUCY (*doing a cowboy imitation*): Yes-sir-ee, pilgrim! I hee-ee-rd of 'em. Them's fightin' words! (*The audience chuckles.*)

SPEAKER (*smiling, chuckling*): Yes, they are fightin' words. But where are they used?

MARK: Those are the words used for splitting congregations.

LUCY: They're used to fire seminary professors.

JOHN: They were used against my congregation twelve years ago.

SPEAKER: And what happens to communities of faith when all that's left is fightin' words?

LUCY: There goes the neighborhood! (*The audience chuckles.*)

SPEAKER: Exactly! When people start using that kind of language, the village gets bombed. And how are these actions justified?

AUDIENCE MEMBER: It's God's will.

SPEAKER: Yes. It's God's will. God is blamed for what leadership does to the sheep. So, what are these words that divide and make people nuts? Where did they come from, and when did people start to use them? What were the circumstances, and could they be a product of trauma? Are these fightin' words just one more example of blank-wall-bowing post-trauma reaction? (*The speaker pauses.*)

The second story involving these words is a story not mentioned in your materials. This story is also centuries old. It illustrates how post-trauma reaction can dictate church politics, relationships, and organizational structure. And it happens even today.

Many of our organizational structures are the products of post trauma reactions, reactions from unprocessed, un-integrated, and sometimes very old trauma—trauma that continues to interfere with creative, logical, empathetic problem solving and decision-making.

This second story involves a group of Protestant churches, a group that moved from Europe to America. They had been abused by princes who reached a compromise to end all the fighting among the different churches. The princes wanted an end to all church conflicts.

Their solution was to have only one church, a combined church, a united church. And all people would believe the same things, say the same prayers, and have the same doctrines. Everyone would have to speak the same message that is consistent with the teachings of that new, united church.

No longer could they speak their own confessions of faith or use their own words, for they were now all members of the one, unified church.

But a group of Protestants went before the princes and said, "We will not accept your watered-down compromises. We will not obey your commands nor give up our doctrines, our own *words*. Our conscience is held captive to the Word of God. We will not jeopardize our eternal salvation! We must obey God rather than man. Therefore, we cannot live in this land. We will leave."

"Fine," said the princes. "You can leave this land. But your property, that belongs to the state. You cannot take anything with you."

"Fine," replied the Protestants. "You can have all the properties. We are leaving."

"Oh, and by the way," replied the princes, "*das geld*—your money—that, too, belongs to the state. You must leave that too."

"Fine," said the Protestants. "You can have your money. We must obey God rather than man."

"Oh," said the princes, "there is one more thing you have to leave."

"What is there left to leave?" asked the Protestants. "You already have everything we own."

"*Deine kinderin*," replied the princes, "your children. They too belong to the state. You must also leave them behind."

I cannot judge these Protestants for their decision to leave their country. They left for the New World, America, with nothing aside from their faithfulness to their beliefs, faith, and words. (*He pauses.*) And so, armed with the we-must-obey-God-rather-than-man resolve, they set sail for the New World, leaving their hearts behind.

Now what would you call what happened to these Protestants?

AUDIENCE: Terrible! Awful! How could they do it?

LUCY: Trauma!

SPEAKER: In a word, trauma. Now what would you be like from that point on?

MARK: This is beyond words. I really don't see how they would Ever...ever go on.

SPEAKER: They did go on—to the New World. And when they arrived, they soon found other Protestants just like themselves, who claimed to follow the same confessions, doctrines, and the same words.

But suddenly, these traumatized Europeans reacted in horror to those American Protestants who had abandoned their native tongue, who dared to speak the sacred words ... in English! They had changed their words!

"*Nein! Nein! Nein!*" screamed the traumatized Europeans. "You have compromised the Word of God. You are not true to the confessions. You have jeopardized your own salvation. We must obey God rather than man!" And so they all ran from the American Protestants, who were left shocked and surprised. What question do you think the American Protestants asked?

LUCY: "Who were those masked men?" (*The audience laughs.*)

SPEAKER (*waiting for audience*): That's probably pretty close.

Those poor American Protestants never knew what hit 'em. They had no clue as to why these newly arrived people ran out of a perfectly sound building, screaming like Casper's evil twin had gone a-haunting! (*The audience chuckles.*)

And so the traumatized European Protestants fled from the confused American Protestants, just like they had fled from the European princes, simply because the Americans did not speak their words. Such language differences were enough to trigger a post-trauma reaction, a flight reaction. And so they took off.

Now was that trauma ever debriefed? Was it processed? Is it now a source of identity and strength? Is it still around? Are there Protestant churches today that use these same words, these fightin' words, to frame their discussions?

MARK: Of course! We all know those words. Been in enough church fights.

SPEAKER: Exactly! Even after generations and generations, overtures from other Christians who believe the same creeds and have the same doctrines are still greeted with the same post-trauma flight reaction. The battle cry of this group remains

"Unless you say it the way we say it, unless you use the exact same words we use to say the same thing, unless you say it just like us, *you have compromised the Word of God, you are not true to the confessions and doctrines, you have jeopardized your eternal salvation,* and *we must obey God rather than man.*" (*He pauses.*) Now what message are these people giving the world?

AUDIENCE MEMBER: Say it our way, or go pound salt! (*The audience amens.*)

SPEAKER: Is that the message God wants us to send? (*long pause*) Is there a difference between the post-trauma reactions of forcing others to bow to blank walls and forbidding people to use their own words? What would you call it?

AUDIENCE MEMBER 1: Odd!

AUDIENCE MEMBER 2: Strange!

AUDIENCE MEMBER 3: Unbelievable!

SPEAKER: Do these words sound familiar? Remind you of an exercise we all did earlier?

JOHN: Okay, okay, I get it. We all do odd stuff. But how did they get each new generation to buy into that mindset, especially since we live in a country with freedom of speech?

SPEAKER: Good question. How would these folks continue their odd and strange ways, ways that make no sense?

JOHN: They would have to (*realization dawning*)...they would have to...to leave their brains and hearts at the church door.

SPEAKER: That sounds like a sign.

JOHN, MARK, AND LUCY: It is a sign!

JOHN: It's *my* sign!

SPEAKER: Maybe you should patent it.

JOHN: Who would buy it?

SPEAKER (*pausing*): Unfortunately, many church leaders would love to hang it around the necks of the sheep. (*There is dead silence in the room.*) Well, now that I've brought this house down (*The audience nervously laughs.*), are there any questions? (*His voice fades out.*) Yes, question in the back row...

JOHN: (*whispering*): It's just so scary...scary to see this being done to the sheep—and in God's name. Really, really...scary.

MARK (*whispering back*): Scary more to Lucy and me.

JOHN: Oh? Why is that?

MARK: Hell is reserved for the shepherds, not the sheep.

JOHN: Oh really?

LUCY: Yep. The prophets said, "Woe to you shepherds of the sheep."

MARK: And Jesus said to the leadership, "You have made these people twice as fit for hell as you are yourselves!"

JOHN: So if shepherds have reservations in hell, why in the world do you want *me* to become one of *you*?

LUCY AND MARK (*looking at each other, then looking at John*): Misery loves company! (*Both burst out laughing.*)

JOHN (*shaking his head*): You love me. You both really, really love me!

SPEAKER: Okay, once again, great questions! We have some time limits, so are you ready for another church trauma story? (*Crowd reacts: "Go for it!"*) Okay, the story of the European Protestants' descendants goes on.

This story, the third story for today, occurred a generation ago.

A generation ago, some church leaders who were descendants of those who had resisted and left Europe were again triggered into a post-trauma reaction. Such reactions are triggered by the activities of their own seminary professors. These seminary professors chose to engage in creative, logical dialogue with other Protestants instead of walking out of discussions when the other Christians did not use their language, their frameworks, or their words.

LUCY (*whispering*): Horror of horrors! Having a conversation with *heathens*!

MARK (*whispering*): The "churchocrats" probably blew a gasket.

SPEAKER: As a result of not walking out, the centuries-old buried trauma was triggered. In post-trauma reaction, the leaders threatened their own seminary professors for not running away from these fake Christians who did not use the right words. Now what did the leadership say to their own professors who dialogued with other Christians? All together now...

SPEAKER ANDAUDIENCE: "You have compromised the Word of God", "You are unfaithful to the doctrines", "You have jeopardized your own salvation", and "We must obey God rather than man".

SPEAKER: And guess what happened to the seminary professors?

MARK: They fled!

SPEAKER: Yes, they did flee, along with many congregations.

AUDIENCE MEMBER: So what happened to them?

SPEAKER: The breakaway churches defiantly broke the rule, the "Do not talk to other Protestants" rule.

LUCY (*whispering*): Dammed for sure!

SPEAKER: And they continued to talk with other Protestants until they found common ground. They discovered that they could say the same things, using different words, without compromising the Word of God, being unfaithful to the confessions, or jeopardizing anyone's salvation.

JOHN (*whispering*): That was a stretch!

SPEAKER: And so they found two other groups of Protestants, and the three groups fell in love. There was a marriage proposal to merge. But just as they got to the altar, the breakaway Protestants nearly fled—again—because of a discussion of power. They reacted to the sharing of power with the bishops. Now what reason could there be for them to flee from discussing the bishops' power?

LUCY: Are you joking?

SPEAKER: I never joke about power—to a Wolverine! (*The audience chuckles.*)

AUDIENCE MEMBER: The breakaway Protestants had just experienced tyranny. Of course, they would flee. That was their history.

AUDIENCE MEMBER 2: The breakaways would run from any bishop with any power.

SPEAKER: And that would be called…all together now! SPEAKER ANDAUDIENCE: Post-trauma reaction!

SPEAKER: Give yourselves a high five! And what would be the odds of pulling off this merger if the other two churches didn't back down from the bishops' power?

AUDIENCE: None!

SPEAKER: Exactly! Oh, they tried dialoguing, negotiating, but the bishops' power had to go. There could be no creative, logical conversation with the post-trauma-reactive breakaway group. But to everyone's surprise, the merger happened.

AUDIENCE (*reacting*): No way! How? Didn't happen!

SPEAKER: Oh, it did happen. They got to the altar, and they all said "I do."

Anyone know the vows they said to each other?

MARK: "That which unites us is greater than that which divides us."

SPEAKER: That sounds like someone who's seen those vows before.

MARK: Our denomination has the patent. (*The audience chuckles.*)

AUDIENCE MEMBER 1: So does ours! (*more chuckling*)

AUDIENCE MEMBER 2: Ours too! (*The audience laughs.*)

SPEAKER (*waiting for audience*): But what happened to the bishops' power?

AUDIENCE MEMBER 3: Didn't happen. Dead on arrival! 97

SPEAKER: Dead on! The bishops lost all power, but they got married anyway. And most of the congregation of the newly merged church had no idea that they had lost their partner. There was no longer a shared partnership between congregations and their bishops.

And so congregations were out there alone to face the wolf in shepherd's clothing. Even if there was proof of wrongdoing, abuse of power, or questionable ethics, the bishop could do nothing. A bishop could not investigate or intervene, despite the outcry of the traumatized, unless the church council formally voted to invite the bishop to the church. But even if the bishop accepts the invitation, the church council could reject any or all of the bishop's recommendations.

As a result, more congregations were traumatized. And for much longer, by church leadership itself, both lay and clergy. The investigations once made by the bishops based on reports from congregations couldn't be done anymore. The merged church lost an important piece of systemic account-ability—a piece lost to post trauma reaction.

Are there any questions before I give the groups their assignments? (*People raise their hands; voices fade.*)

MARK (*whispering back and forth*): That's...that's ridiculous! Is that how it happened?

LUCY: I can't believe it! We lost the office of bishop to post-trauma reaction?

JOHN: I'm so mad, I can't...you mean, all those times I talked to the bishop—all the visits, the documentation, the begging to have an investigation—and all the while, nothing could be done!

LUCY: Sh-h-h-h, John, keep it down. But you are right. Nothing could be done.

JOHN: Because of what happened four hundred years ago? MARK: Sh-h-h. Yes, and forty years ago.

JOHN: But the council was full of his sycophants, Kool-Aid drinkers who jumped whenever he(*realization dawning*)... Oh God, he knew this! He knew we couldn't touch him. That's why he stacked the council with his people, the charmed!

LUCY: That's the way it's done, especially if you are a narcissist control freak.

JOHN: So he was brave enough to threaten, lie, steal, or do whatever to us because he knew nothing could be done. He would not be held accountable no matter what. He had the council votes, so the bishop couldn't investigate. And so he got away with it. For seven looong years, he got away with it! And there was nothing, *nothing*, we could do about it—not one thing! No wonder he had a plastic grin pasted on his face!

LUCY: Okay, okay, John. We'll talk later. The Q and A is nearly over. Let's see about the assignment.

SPEAKER: Thank you for your questions. And now, for the assignments. First, take the odd behavior you identified in the first session and start asking questions. Get curious. Ask the questions you may have been afraid to ask. Questions like,

> When did you begin to notice your odd behaviors?
> What was going on at the time?
> What did you do, say, or feel at that time?
> What were the painful words that you've said to yourself?
> When did you start saying it?

Now the statements you used to tell yourself need not *be* true or rational. The statements just have to *feel* true, which has nothing to do with reality or intelligence.

When my spouse was dying, it felt true that I was a lousy spouse for not being able to help, cure, or control the cancer. Those self-eviscerating statements came from the unprocessed pictures of pain and powerlessness throwing me into post-trauma reaction. I was in a movie, a bad horror movie, looping round and round…seeing the suffering, feeling the suffering…over and over.

After the funeral, just about anything and everything seemed to trigger these horrible mental images. Until these images were debriefed, processed, and integrated into my awareness, I could not see nor grieve over my lost. I could not see the reality behind this heroic battle waged against cancer. I could not see the truth of the blessings that this one solitary life had given to me, to our children, and to all the children in the community.

Therefore, in your groups of three, use those odd behaviors and get curious, deeply curious, and search for truth—your own truth, trauma's truth. Ask all the questions mentioned above. Look close and deep.

You can take your time and use your lunch period to continue the conversations. But before you go, I have two important reminders. First, keep in mind the two very important words. Anyone know the most often quoted words in the Bible?

LUCY: Fear not!

SPEAKER: Yes, fear not. Why am I not surprised, Lucy?

LUCY: 'Cause we, Wolverines, are *fearless!* (*The audience chuckles.*)

SPEAKER: Yes, you are. "Fear not" is very important. Whenever God shows up, we can fear not. Whenever there are two or three gathered in God's name, we can fear not.

You can also fear not because you have faced the trauma and survived. You're alive because you used your God-given survival skills, and they worked. You made it! You're here!

You can also fear not because you have each other, in God's name. Even though it feels awful to go into the backyard of your mind, to the toxic waste sites, you can trust each other with whatever you find. The same way as you are trusted by God.

You can also fear not because trauma experts are present and available for conversations.

And last but most importantly, you can fear not because the Traumatized One, the one crucified and traumatized for everyone of us, already knows your trauma. He is always ready to redeem it, to raise it up from its backyard burial, and for its learnings to be your teacher as you follow Him.

And the second reminder is this. Take care of each other as God has taken care of you.

See you later this afternoon.

Discussion Questions

1. What do you make of the church whose members used to bow to a blank wall? What kind of witness did that church give to the world? If you had gone to that church,

    a) what questions would you pursue, regardless of the pushback and pressure not to ask such questions?

b) how would you intellectually justify the practice of bowing and your compliance to it?

c) would you be able to never return to the church and tell others of the negative experience?

2. Two questions were asked in order to diagnose if the church is in post trauma reaction: When did the odd behavior appear and what happened just before the odd behavior appeared? How can those questions help in diagnosing the trauma?

3. How do you think the following accusations have affected relationships within the faith communities and toward other faith communities:

"You have compromised the word of God, unfaithful to the confessions/doctrines of the church, jeopardized your own salvation, so we must obey God rather than man?"

Are these really "fightin' words," as Lucy described?

Possible Responses to DQ

1. They were conditioned, they had their own little quirk that contained no explaining, to which none of them bothered to ask about. But they did it nonetheless, because that was what they were told to do. It would probably have been better to be confrontational and ask questions regarding this wall, rather than complying blindly on something that was purely a mystery to you. Even God himself was never this mysterious.

   If given a chance, I would ask the same questions that the were taught in the conference. Also, I can't seem to think of any intellectual interpretation of the odd practice, unless I look closer and deeper into the church's history. If

I have been manipulated to do the same bowing practice, I doubt that I would be able to leave the church and share the odd bowing-to-the-blank-wall.

2. The questions help us develop a deeper understanding of our odd behaviors. By identifying what it is, and figuring out what happened right before, it helps us deduce whether there actually was a traumatic event that occurred and what triggered the odd behavior.

3. It triggers fear and anxiety among the people within the congregations. As Lucy called them, these are indeed fighting words, because they induce an attack towards the people, regarding their faith and stance as a person of the church. It violates the people trust and confidence in themselves—their gut feelings and deductions.

CHAPTER 7

Touchstone Events

*Are you an open book? Or are you the silent type? Would you feel
comfortable sharing your thoughts, emotions, and experiences? What
about your biggest fears, and the darkest experiences that you had?
Do you think sharing such things would make a difference in you?*

Commentary

Let me share a recipe for church trauma. It reads as follows:

Take one package of narcissism. Place narcissism in a large bowl
and sip accountability out. .Narcissism already contains enough of
those.

Then add one measure of refined wit and two measures of
obvious intelligence. Stir vigorously while continuously adding "You
compromised the Word of God" with "You are unfaithful to the doctrines". Carefully add pinches of "You are jeopardizing your salvation" with a dash of "We must obey God rather than man." Add these
ingredients slowly because putting them too quickly may induce an
attack of creative and logical thinking within the congregation.

Let the concoction cook in the heat of the persistent belief that
"God wants me to be in charge", "The whole world revolves around
me", and "Anyone else opposing me is really opposing God."

Be sure to serve in small servings, slowly. It only takes one small serving to achieve an immediate, cascading church trauma.

If such dish is not processed and excreted, expect the congregation to experience a long-lasting trauma. The post-trauma reaction will continue for years—rendering the church lifeless and tasteless. If, on the other hand, the meal undergoes continual processing, or the ingredients are replaced with real teachings and the real calling of the Traumatized One, then expect the trauma to be turned into learning, learning that would be useful not just in the present, but also for the future.

Reader's Theatre

Act 2: Scene 4: Unearthing Burial Sites

MARK: Fear not...fear not? Fear not?!

LUCY: That's what was said, Mark.

JOHN: I don't think I can do this.

MARK: Not by ourselves.

LUCY: That's for sure. But we can do it together (*She looks at the two of them.*)...together!...I hope.

MARK: Well, you're the one who said, "All for one...

JOHN: And one for all!" (*He pauses.*) But are you sure? We can sneak out the back and no one will ever know that we're not—

LUCY (*interrupting*): No, no, no! I'm not giving it up that easy—not without a fight!

MARK: A fight? What are you fighting?

LUCY: Myself! I'm fighting me 'cause I want to run. Eat and run, eat and run. That's all I've ever done. Eat and run. (*She pauses.*) And then tell jokes while I eat and run. Well, *no more!* I'm sick...sick and tired of being...being...

JOHN: Of being sick and tired?

LUCY: Yes!

JOHN: Well, I'm sick and tired of Maggie and the kids walking on eggshells every time I come home from church meetings. I need to face this…this…whatever it is that's causing me to lose control. (*He looks at Lucy and Mark.*) And there's nobody else I'd rather face it other than with you both.

LUCY: Why, John, what a nice, warm fuzzy! Thank you. (*She tries to hug both, but initially Mark pulls away.*)

MARK (*reluctantly agreeing to the hug*): Okay, okay. I'm trapped, but I might as well be trapped…with *two* fuzzies! (*All laugh.*)

JOHN: Okay, okay. Down to business. Who's the first speaker and—

MARK (*interrupting*): I'll go first!

LUCY: Sold to the gentleman in the black collar with a white tab!

JOHN: And I'll be the first observer.

LUCY: Oh, batting cleanup, are we? So-o-o, I'm game. Bring it, Mark!

MARK: Bring what?

LUCY: The kitchen sink—what else? No-o-o, the questions. We're supposed to ask questions about our odd behavior, "when did you notice it, what you say to yourself about it, what was going on when you first noticed it, what is the truth behind it, when did you"—

MARK (*interrupting*): Okay, okay, I get it. I get it! *I get it!* (*He breathes heavily.*) I'm sorry, Lucy. I…just…just felt…

LUCY: Felt trapped?

MARK: Yeah.

LUCY: Pressed a little?

MARK: Yeah. Sorry…for yelling.

LUCY: No need, Mark. But I'm not stepping around any of your… your elephants.

MARK: No, don't. Don't step around! This pachyderm has been parked on my chest for too long (*He rubs his chest then stops.*)…taking up too much space. (*He takes a deep breath.*) Well, here it goes…

JOHN: We're with you, Mark.

MARK: Okay. (*He pauses.*) I've always been scared of small spaces and dark places.

LUCY: Even as a small child?

MARK: Yeah.

LUCY: Even at six years old?

MARK: Yeah (*thinking about it*)...well, no. (*He thinks some more.*) Not at six. I remember from about eight years old, needing a night-light, the bedroom door kept open, but not at six. Hm-m-m...

LUCY: Well, did anything happen after age six? Trapped somewhere in the dark?

MARK: No. (*long pause*) Well, there was a time some older boys pranked us.

LUCY: Pranked you? What do you mean, "pranked" you?

MARK: Well, the older boys wanted nothing to do with us little ones, until one day they invited us to go with them and explore the cement drainage tunnels.

LUCY: And you went. Did you tell your parents?

MARK: No, nobody ever found out...no one, until now.

LUCY (*long pause*): You've never talked about this to anyone?

MARK: No one.

LUCY: Huh. Something happened in the tunnel?

MARK: Yeah. When they got us down in the dark part, they turned off their flashlights, and then they threw cherry bombs at us.

LUCY (*her voice starting to quiver*): Mark, you're in the tunnel...in the dark...with bombs?

MARK: And it was great fun to the older boys, laughing at us younger ones. We bawled our eyes out, screaming, "Mommy! Mommy!" I was so scared I just knew I was going to die. (*He starts to tremble.*)

JOHN (*breathing deeply*): Oh, Mark.

LUCY: I'm so sorry. That poor little guy!

MARK: But when they finally turned the flashlights on, I was crying so hard that snot ran down my face. But the older boys sang, "Fairies, fairies! Tinker Bell fairies! Go home and tell your mommies. Fairies, fairies!" (*He is tearful, wipes his eyes, puts his head down, and takes a long pause.*)

LUCY (*long pause, reaching out*): Mark? Mark? You okay?

MARK (raising his head, pausing): I'm just feeling...feeling...the same terror...ashamed...so afraid—so out of control...like

I was back in the tunnel…humiliated. And the louder they sang, the harder I cried all the way home.

LUCY: And you told no one?

MARK: I couldn't. I just…just hid…hid from everyone because it was my fault.

LUCY: Your fault? How was it your fault?

MARK: Mom and Dad told me never, never, never go in those drainage tunnels. My dad said, "If Jesus came off the cross and told you to go down to the tunnels, don't go!"

LUCY: And you went anyway…you disobeyed God…

MARK: So it was *my fault*—my own stupid fault.

LUCY (*becoming tearful*): That poor little guy trapped in that dark tunnel never had a chance. He got conned…all terrified.

MARK: I remember screaming in my head, "I'm gonna die! I'm gonna die! I'll never see my family again. They'll never find me down here, *and it's all my fault!*" Trapped in that small space—I was so terrified… It was so dark. (*He pauses, realization dawning.*) I never want to go there ever again—not ever—not even in conversations that trap me and leave me…in the dark.

LUCY: I had no idea.

MARK: Neither did I, until this very moment. I never connected the tunnel with my reactions to small and dark places. It's like… like I'm in a movie.

LUCY: How do you feel now?

MARK: I feel… I feel…feel like I'm definitely scheduling with a trauma expert. I need to process this, learn from it and use it so I can help myself and free some other trapped soul too. I need to get out of this movie. Thank you, Lucy, for helping me find it.

LUCY: Find what?

MARK: The truth—my own truth.

LUCY: Thank you, Mark. I'm just so glad you made it out of that tunnel.

MARK: Not yet.

LUCY: What do you mean, "not yet"?

MARK: I'm not out, but I'm seeing some light at…at…

Mark and Lucy: At the end of the tunnel! (*All three laugh and then pause.*)

Lucy: You okay to continue?

Mark: Yeah. It's kind of a relief. At least I know I'm not nuts.

John (*pausing*): That...that was amazing. Just amazing! It felt like I was on...on holy ground.

Lucy: Just keep your shoes on, pal. I'm up next, and *you* are *my* listener!

John: Okay, right! Let's get started. Your odd behavior was fast-eating.

Lucy: Greased lightning without the grease!

John: So when did you notice that was happening?

Lucy: Just like Mark, I thought I always ate fast. But as Mark talked, I realized that's not true. I remember when I ate normally with my friends and cousins, slow enough to talk, have fun while eating, and spend sometime for a visit.

John: But all of it changed.

LUCY: Yes, it did...for some reason.

John: Do you remember where it changed?

Lucy: *Where* it changed? Like a specific place?

John: Yes, a place like...like...

Lucy: The dining room.

John: The dining room?

Lucy: Yes. I started to avoid the dining room.

John: Something happened in the dining room. Something scared you?

Lucy: No (*tears starting to form*). I wasn't scared. I was...was angry— so angry. It made me cry.

John: Something really angered you...in the dining room.

Lucy: Yeah. So I quit eating.

John: You quit eating?

LUCY: Yep. Quit eating with the family...wouldn't come to the dining room until everyone else was done. I sat at the dining room table all by myself. Then I could eat, but not with the family. It became a family joke—but not to me.

John: It was funny to everyone else?

Lucy: Well, my dad...he didn't think it was funny.

JOHN: Your dad was different?

LUCY: Yeah. He couldn't eat very well. He had one of those pockets (*points to her throat*) in his esophagus—a hernia...a...

MARK: A hiatal hernia?

LUCY: Yes, thank you, a hiatal hernia. And food would get stuck in his throat. It gagged him. He sounded like a cat trying to throw a hairball. (She *imitates the cat sound*.) I felt so bad, so sorry for him. Just when we thought it was going down, all of a sudden it would get caught. It just wasn't fair.

JOHN: What wasn't fair?

LUCY (*tears starting to flow*): He tried to eat, but he couldn't. And Mom would yell at him, "You ruined dinner, *again!*" She gave him her daily dose of remedies: "You could help it if you just chewed more, ...ate more vegetables, ...drink milk first." She gave him all kinds of medications, but none worked. So, in the end, she resorted to yelling. My father gagged until he left the table. He'd put his fingers down his throat and puke. We heard him puking as we sat at the dining room table... trying to eat. How I hated that table!

JOHN: Is that when you stopped eating at the table?

LUCY: Yeah. After puking, Dad would go downstairs and sit by himself in the basement. That basement—all by himself. Everyone else was still upstairs at...at that dining room table.

JOHN: But you weren't in the dining room?

LUCY: No. I went downstairs to the basement to be with him, to cheer him up, to make him...to make him...laugh. (*Realization dawns.*) Oh my!

JOHN: What?

LUCY: That's why I wouldn't eat at the table with the family. *I wanted to be with him*—to make him laugh, to make him feel better. So, when everyone left, I went back upstairs and wolfed down leftovers, like I was on fire ...like...like...

JOHN: Like greased lightning.

MARK: But without the grease.

LUCY: Yes. But it was my fault—*my fault!* If I were just a better kid, a better daughter, God would make Daddy feel better...and Mommy wouldn't be so mean to him! (*Hot tears flow.*)

JOHN: But God didn't help.

LUCY: No, God didn't help *because I failed!* A failure at nine, because I couldn't cure my dad and couldn't control my mom. I blamed myself for causing the mess. All I wanted to do was eat, eat normally. But I was scared. I just wanted to get away—away from that...that table...that war zone!

JOHN: Still is...

LUCY: Yeah.

JOHN: Still fighting, every meal is a battle...

LUCY: Yeah.

JOHN: Eating...

LUCY: Yeah, still in the movie.

JOHN: Using your humor to make us all feel better and laugh. But the cost is...

LUCY: Can't afford it. I'm done paying! Move over, Mark. I'm in line for a trauma expert. All that counseling, and the truth was obvious, so obvious. I can't go on eating and running and joking. Too painful. *No more!*

JOHN: You survived.

LUCY: I survived *then. Now* I want *to live.* (*She takes a Kleenex and blows her nose.*)

JOHN: You okay?

LUCY (*speaking in a thick Eastern European accent, while pinching her nose with the Kleenex*): Yes, but no jokes for you!

MARK: Ha! Well, I'm glad you survived the war at the dining room table.

LUCY: And I'm glad you got out of that tunnel.

JOHN (*long pause*): I think by a process of elimination...

LUCY AND MARK: It's your turn, buddy!

JOHN: Okay, okay. (*He arranges to sit in the speaker's chair.*) But isn't it time for lunch?

LUCY: Not a chance!

MARK: It's a miracle that you are here, John. Thank you again for... volunteering.

JOHN: Yeah. Just like volunteering...in the military!

MARK: You were in the military?

JOHN: Did a four-year stint. The military helped me discover two things about myself.

MARK: Oh yeah? What were they?

JOHN: First, I don't like military life. And second, I am a sheep dog.

LUCY AND MARK: A what?

JOHN: A sheep dog. I'm a sheep dog.

MARK: What do you mean?

JOHN: A sheep dog protects and defends the sheep with his life. In the military, we don't have the luxury of being sheep. We, sheep dogs, are the protectors, the defenders. The sheep just don't get us, don't even like us. We see the danger before sheep do and take care of business—even at a huge cost.

MARK: And what did it cost you twelve years ago?

JOHN: What?

MARK: Twelve years ago you protected and defended the sheep, from the wolf.

JOHN: Good God! Was that what I was doing?

MARK: Did you complete your mission, soldier?

JOHN (*bolting up and standing at attention*): No, no, sir! I did not complete my mission, sir. I was outmanned, outmaneuvered...could not directly engage the enemy, sir! (*significant pause, looking down*)

I failed to protect the sheep. It was my fault. I underestimated his level of evil, his disregard for the sheep, and willingness to do any means necessary to serve his own purposes. (*He pauses again.*) I deserve no mercy, no forgiveness, no grace, sir!

MARK: The enemy was cunning, baffling, and powerful.

JOHN: But it happened on my watch—*my watch!*

MARK: Your watch?

JOHN: My watch! As a council member, it was my job to protect the flock, to bring order out of chaos—and I paid for it!

MARK: At what cost, soldier?

JOHN: The cost was loss of sleep, loss of a safe place to worship, lost peace of mind.

MARK: But those weren't the biggest costs, were they, soldier?

JOHN: No, sir.

MARK: The cost was your home.

JOHN: Yes, sir.

MARK: You brought the fight into your house.

JOHN: Yes, s-sir. (*voice cracking with emotion*)

MARK: And you were angered.

JOHN: Yes, s-s-ir-r-r! (*weeping*)

MARK: And you attacked your own little lambs.

JOHN: Yes! Yes! Yes! (*openly sobbing*) I took it out on them—on *my* lambs, my little lambs. I-I told Maggie to sign the divorce papers. But she refused. She wouldn't sign. She kept saying, "You are not responsible for the church," and "We are not the enemy. We. Are not. The enemy."

MARK: Who was the real enemy?

JOHN: No! I can't!

MARK: *Who was the enemy, soldier?*

JOHN: It was me! I became the enemy. I treated Maggie just like how my enemy treated me. I became him! I became him... in my very own home. I became the wolf, the wolf to my own sheep. Nasty, mean, controlling—manipulating to get my own way, and threatening to leave if I didn't get *my way*!

MARK: He humiliated you...

JOHN: Yes.

MARK: That you had compromised the Word of God.

JOHN: Yes.

MARK: Unfaithful...

JOHN: Yes.

MARK: And if you didn't shut up, you would jeopardize everyone's eternal salvation.

JOHN: Yes, yes, and yes!

MARK: But you didn't shut up.

JOHN: No, sir! I am a sheep dog. I did not leave my post, sir.

MARK: You did not leave the sheep.

JOHN: No, sir. I did not leave the sheep. I kept my watch. But he publicly humiliated, ridiculed all of us with "You are taking man's ways, not God's"—trying to get us to...to...

MARK: To park your brains and hearts at the door?

JOHN (*realization dawning*): Yes! Yes! To follow him...to follow him—blind, deaf, and dumb.

MARK: Like sheep?

JOHN: Yes, just like sheep led to the slaughter.

MARK: But you didn't shut up.

JOHN: No, sir! I would not let him devour the sheep—not without a fight. *But I failed.*

MARK: You fought well, soldier. Because of your suffering, the church still stands. But you never suffered alone, because the Traumatized One was with you.

JOHN: But Maggie and the kids...

MARK: They suffered.

JOHN: Yes.

MARK: They suffered, you suffered, the church suffered.

JOHN: Yes.

MARK: And Jesus suffered...with all of you.

JOHN (*long pause*): But I could've...should've...done something.

MARK: You should've done something else?

JOHN: But...but I did everything—everything I could.

MARK: That was not enough.

JOHN: It wasn't enough, but...but...there was nothing left to do.

MARK (*pausing*): There is only one thing left to do.

JOHN: What's that?

MARK: *Come home!* It's time to come home, soldier.

JOHN: Come home?

MARK: The flock lives. You are still husband and dad. *Come home!*

JOHN: I don't deserve it. I'm... I'm just a...a failure.

LUCY: John, you're a survivor, just like we are. You are forgiven. Come home.

JOHN: That's a lot to forgive.

LUCY: It is not that much for God. Come home, John.

MARK: You are not alone. You are here, with us, looking for healing.

JOHN (*long pause*): Yeah, you're right. I get it. LUCY AND MARK: Get what?

JOHN: I get why I'm here—with the two of you...in this place. I'm here for healing, to clean out the backyard of my mind. And to finally recycle it.

MARK: Recycle it?

JOHN: Yeah, recycle it. I'm going to take this mental compost pile I've been living in for twelve years and recycle it so that I can... can...

MARK: Can be raised?

JOHN: Yeah. To a new life! With a little help (*looking at Mark and Lucy*) from my friends.

MARK: Well, where two or three are gathered...

LUCY: There's always a resurrection!

JOHN: A resurrection—but not without a conversation with that trauma expert. Move over, guys! I'm scheduling in!

LUCY (*singing*): We-e-e're off to see the wizard! The wonderful wizard of...

Discussion Questions

1. Mark, Lucy, and John connected the dots between their odd behaviors and their trauma history. Why would that be scary? What do you make of God telling us, "Fear not" throughout the Bible? What would make it safe enough for you to self disclose?

2. How did the three people treat each other while each of them spoke? What feelings do you notice in you as they processed their stories? Would you feel safe enough to disclose your pain to one of these people? Why or why not?

3. Which of the stories resonates with you? What was it like to hear each person's trauma? Does any of the stories remind you of your own trauma? Have you ever considered getting assistance for trauma recovery?

Possible Responses to DQ

1. It would be scary because they would be facing the fears that they themselves were not aware of before. Eventually, their speech made them talk even more about unrealized fears—and the trauma that shakes us to the bone. But God understands us because His bones were broken, His body was given, His blood was shed, for us. For us, God was also shaken to the bone and therefore, God is able to enter our bone shaken space, saying to us, "Be not afraid ... For Lo, I am with you always." And because God is with us, God gives us the gift of courage, even in the face of our fears. And there is no shortage of courage from God for those willing to receive it. Therefore, we can explore and learn from those scary places of the past, because we do not go alone.

2. They showed understanding and open-mindedness to each other, all while making humorous and light-hearted statements in order to help make each other comfortable. All three of them know when to situate the humor and joke around, and are open enough to listen whenever the situation calls for seriousness. They are fairly good listeners and are amazing at making each other feel heard, which would make them great people to disclose emotions to.

3. All three of them were familiar stories, all of which unlocked deep memories for myself, and most likely for many of the readers of this book. Trauma resolution should never be second-guessed; the moment you think you need it confirms the provoking thought.

CHAPTER 8:

A New Beginning

Have you ever overcome a fear or any embarrassing habits or behaviors before? Have you experienced achieving something that seemed to be unattainable? Have you ever accomplished one thing that you once thought you could never do? If so, how did you feel afterwards? Who were the people who were with you along the way? And what resources did you take advantage of?

Commentary

Making that first connection between the odd, strange, embarrassing behavior, and one's past trauma is liberating: "At last, I'm connecting the dots. It's not in my DNA to be weird. I'm reacting to being in a buried movie. I'm not strange. It's not who I am!"

Seeing the connection is the initial, and probably most crucial, step in post-trauma growth. Through the connection, you can develop a language framework. Consequently, the language framework reduces anxiety by making post-trauma reactions meaningful. Like, "At last, it finally makes sense!"

This connection also gives a measure of comfort—a glimmer of hope that maybe "I'm not bad, weak, stupid, crazy, a failure, not enough, or guilty." However, that realization is just at the intellectual level. The healing happens much deeper, at the feeling-sensing-body level.

For that healing to begin, the toxic trauma sites buried in the mental backyard need a serious excavation. We have to get out of the grip of rationalizations and religious-sounding justifications to find the stored, unprocessed motion pictures of powerlessness, vulnerability, and loss of control. These memory sites are the hot zones. They are triggered by images, sights, sounds, sensations, situations, and words connected to those pictures.

Through processing and integrating them into our awareness, the energy in the pictures becomes redeemable and available for life, growth, and wise decision-making. Then, it becomes our life teacher. From it, we grow from being trauma survivors and become renewed trauma thrivers, all with more grace and wisdom for living.

Excavating and recycling buried trauma is not that simple, though. Even the most careful attempts to excavate could still trigger post-trauma reactions. Therefore, "it takes a village" for people to help, for people to step out of the energized mental motion pictures so that they can finally see trauma from afar, and not from within themselves.

It takes a village—not just any village—but a village that speaks the language, has a framework, and enters the conversation with the faithful assurance that the Traumatized One is with them each and every step of the way. As Mark's faith statement, "Where two or three are gathered together," means we have a safe place, a sanctuary, a healing place, a trauma village to resurrect and be resurrected together.

On our own, we cannot control ourselves from being triggered. The best we can do by ourselves are (1) avoid the things that trigger us, (2) become very controlling with people, places, and things, or (3) use the right thinking and self-talking, (4)attempt to argue with ourselves to prevent oneself from being triggered. These options, however, only increase internal anxiety and the need for external control. In other words, using these options just make us more cranky, controlling, numb, and alone.

Mark, Lucy, and John all realized that they need a catharsis, a deeper connection and healing than just the awareness of the connected dots. They have chosen to talk with trauma experts, the people who understand how trauma works and how it needs to be addressed. They realize now that they know what they know and cannot "unknow" it anymore. They know just enough to feel miserable.

Therefore, they have to move forward for themselves, for their families, and for the church. They know that inflicting post-trauma reactivity on others just causes more trauma, something they just realized and now refuse to do. Therefore, they are claiming responsibility for their own post-trauma reactions, taking a stand, and seeking help.

The good news is that they are now seeking the help they always needed. They are seeking that help, first, from each other. The more they understand their own trauma and reactivity, the less anxious they feel, and the more helpful they become with each other. They have become willing to enter the trauma conversation and are mutually growing in themselves, their love for each other, and their commitment for further growth. Their trust in themselves and each other has expanded through mutual authenticity, empathy, and transparency. They have become united in healing themselves and each other. They are epitomizing the wisdom of "love your neighbor as yourself."

Can you imagine a whole church engaged in trauma ministry? Is this not what it means to "pick up your cross and follow Me"?

Reader's Theatre

Act 3, Scene 1: A Normal Breakfast

At breakfast the next morning, Mark and Lucy are eating when John joins them.

JOHN: Well, either I'm late, or the two of you are early.
LUCY AND MARK: You're late! (*They laugh.*)
MARK: For the first time in months, I woke up refreshed. Feels great!
LUCY: Me too. It's like…like something new is here—a new day.
JOHN: Thank God for you guys, because my sleep was different too.

MARK: In what way?

JOHN: Well, I dreamed.

LUCY (*pausing, confused*): You dreamed? That's it?

JOHN (*defiantly*): Yeah, I had a dream—a weird dream.

MARK: A nightmare?

JOHN: No. I've had those. But not this time. It was just…weird.

LUCY: Well, are you going to tell us?

JOHN: Only if you promise not to laugh.

LUCY: Can't do that!

MARK (*looking at Lucy*): Oh yes you can! (*He looks at John.*) Come on, John. Spill it!

JOHN: Okay, okay. Well, my dream was about my sign.

MARK AND LUCY: Your sign?

JOHN: Yes, my sign. My church sign, the "Enter at own risk—

LUCY (*interrupting*): "Park your hearts and brains at the door" sign?

MARK: A sign only a bishop could love. (*Mark and Lucy laugh.*)

JOHN: Look, do you want to hear it or not?

LUCY: Pretty please? With sugar substitute on top.

JOHN (*looks at the table then notices Lucy's food*): Hey, you…you're still eating! It's not all gone!

LUCY: Yep. It's a new day.

MARK: Real new! She was no greased lightning; ate at my pace. We had breakfast, for the first time, *together.*

LUCY: I guess I'm no longer the fastest tongue in the West.

MARK AND JOHN: Boo-o-o!

LUCY: Okay, okay, I'll stop.

MARK: Never!

JOHN: But something happened, didn't it?

LUCY: It sure did.

MARK: So are you going to tell us or should we just guess it?

LUCY: You'll never guess! After talking with the trauma expert, on the way back to my room, I had a…a heightened awareness.

JOHN: A heightened awareness?

LUCY: Yes. It was…a moment of clarity. Like stepping out of a…a movie. I could see it, but wasn't in it. I felt more alive, more in tune, with eyes wide open…

MARK: ...To the mercies of God.

LUCY: Yeah. Felt present—grounded. And I owe it all to cheese and crackers!

MARK: Cheese and crackers? You never ate cheese and crackers.

LUCY: And some wine.

JOHN (*pausing*): And you didn't invite us?

LUCY: There was only a little bit left from last night's wine tasting.

MARK: So what happened?

LUCY: I got back to my room, and while on a search-and-destroy mission for food, I accidentally sat on the crackers.

JOHN: Ha, ha! I love Lucy!

LUCY: You think I sat on them on purpose?

JOHN: Well, no. I don't think that you—

LUCY (*interrupting*): And spilled the wine.

MARK: You did what?

LUCY: When I realized that I had butt-smashed the crackers, I jumped up and knocked over the wine.

JOHN: Crushed crackers and spilled wine—blog at eleven!

MARK: That's it?

LUCY: No. The crackers were crushed and scattered; the wine was running all over the table. So I started to clean the table, and that's when it hit.

JOHN: What hit?

LUCY (*begins to tear, voice a little shaky*): The crushed crackers, the crushed body...broken and scattered. The spilled wine...His blood... (*Tearful, she pauses.*)

MARK (*realization dawning*): Oh, go on, Lucy! Please, go on.

LUCY: After cleaning it up, I sat down, closed my eyes, and saw another table, a dining room table. It was like the dining room table where I grew up, but this one was huge. It stretched on and on. And crowds of people were all there. And then I saw... I saw...him. (*crying*)

MARK: Who, Lucy? Who did you see?

LUCY (*trying to compose herself*): I saw- I saw...my poor dad. (*She pauses.*) But Dad was sitting at the dining room table—eating—right next …to Jesus! Both were sitting at the dining room table, eating together.

JOHN: He was eating?

LUCY: He was! He was eating, and he wasn't getting sick.

JOHN: Not the way you remembered him.

LUCY: No. He wasn't choking. He didn't have to leave. No one yelled at him. He was…he was…at peace.

MARK: What a gift! A vision of mercy! A thing of beauty!

LUCY: And then both Dad and Jesus, they both waved me in to sit down next to them. I hesitated, but Dad called me, "C'mon, Lucy. He's prepared a place for us at His dining room table. Come and sit here!" (*She is tearful, but composed.*)

MARK: Awesome—powerful!

LUCY: That table—that terrible dining room table—where dad used to coke and puke. The dining table where Mom used to yell… God has redeemed…redeemed it all—the whole mess! I'm so overwhelmed to be invited to sit and stay at God's dining room table.

JOHN: So vivid, like you're…you're in a new movie, a brand-new movie.

LUCY: Yeah, a replacement movie. The other one stunk. But when I opened my eyes, I was at peace. I was enough. And it was all…okay. (*She looks at the other two, who are looking down. There is a long pause.*) What's the matter? What's wrong?

MARK: Nothing. It's just that…that something similar happened to me.

JOHN: Me too, but it was in my dream.

LUCY: Oh yes, your sign…in the dream. I'm sorry. I just got carried away.

JOHN: Lucy, you've given me courage to share my own moment of clarity. No need to apologize. I'm honored you invited me to your table.

MARK: Me too.

LUCY: Thank you. Thank you both. You are so gracious, so understanding, so…

JOHN: So knock it off, will ya? I'm starting to blush! (*He pauses.*) Now do you want to hear what happened in my dream or not?

LUCY AND MARK (*together*): Yes, please, go on! What happened to the sign? Your dream?

JOHN: You can't laugh.

MARK AND LUCY: John!

JOHN: All right, okay. It's wonderful, but really- really…

LUCY: Really tough?

JOHN: Yeah.

LUCY: John, we love you. So please, go ahead.

JOHN: Okay, but I'll need to borrow some of your courage, Lucy.

LUCY: You take all you want, but just tell us about your dream.

JOHN: Okay, here it goes. (*He pauses.*) In my dream, I was at the church and saw my sign.

MARK: Your "park your brains and hearts" sign?

JOHN: Yeah. I walked toward it, but then I realized I wasn't alone.

MARK: Someone was with you?

JOHN: Well, I didn't see anyone, at first. But it came out of the shadows.

MARK: It? *It* came out of the shadows?

JOHN: He, she, it—I don't know. But it was an angel.

MARK: Really! But how did you know?

JOHN: Mark, when you meet one, you know! It was an angel.

LUCY: Hm-m-m. Well, did the angel say anything?

JOHN: No, not a word.

MARK: No words? No message? (*John shakes his head no.*) Huh. Well, did the angel *do* anything?

JOHN: Yeah. The angel looked at the sign on the church, my sign. The angel then went over to the sign and took it off the door and then…then, the angel hugged me (*He starts to choke up and tear up*)… Then, the angel put thesign…no, placed the sign in my…in my heart… (*Now tearful, Mark and Lucy touch his arm andshoulder. He somewhat composes himself and continues.*) Then I knew that my sign had become God's sign. That God gave me back my heart and mind, bought it back from a tyrant. God redeemed my heart and mind, and then, I woke up. (*He dries his tears.*)

LUCY (*tearfully*): Oh, John! That was just…just beautiful.

MARK: You're coming home, my friend.

JOHN: And when I woke up, I didn't feel like…like I had failed. I didn't feel like I had failed to protect the sheep from the wolf. I had stood up as a witness… I was faithful—not successful, but faithful.

LUCY: You kept the faith, baby.

JOHN: And what's more, I was forgiven, forgiven for what I did to Maggie.

LUCY (*in wonderment*): Another miracle!

JOHN: It was like…like a noose dropped off my neck.

MARK: A noose?

JOHN: Yes, a noose. (*He gestures with his hand above his head, holding a rope.*) It just…just fell off my throat.

LUCY (*now composed, smiling*): And now, no noose is really good ne-ew-s-s!

MARK AND JOHN (*There is a big pause as they look at each other and then speak to Lucy.*): Lucy! No noose is good news? Are you kidding me?

LUCY: I just couldn't resist—and I'm not sorry.

JOHN: There, but for the grace of God, go…

LUCY: Us! Together! Right, guys?

MARK: All for one…

JOHN: Yep!

LUCY: Right! But Mark, what about you?

MARK: I didn't have any dreams, no signs, but I did draw a picture.

JOHN: A picture? You drew a picture? A picture of what?

MARK: A cave.

LUCY: A cave? You drew a picture of a cave?

MARK: Yes. After the session where they used the eye movement technique, the trauma expert suggested that I draw a picture of what I feared the most: small spaces, dark places. So I drew a picture of a cave.

LUCY: Just a cave?

MARK: No, not just any cave. I drew *the* cave.

JOHN: *The* cave? What cave?

LUCY: The cave in the garden?

MARK: Yes.

LUCY: Where Jesus was buried?

MARK: Yes.

LUCY: And what did it look like?

MARK: It was dark, small…

LUCY: What did you do after you finished drawing it?

MARK: I looked at the darkness and went inside.

LUCY: Inside the cave?

MARK: Yeah, inside.

JOHN: But you don't do crawl spaces, let alone tombs!

MARK: I had to go in.

JOHN AND LUCY: Why? Why did you go in?

MARK: Because He called me. He called me into the cave. JOHN AND
LUCY: Who? Who called you in?

MARK (*looking at both of them, incredulous*): Who's buried in Grant's
tomb?

LUCY: Martin Luther! (*Mark looks at Lucy, tilts then shakes* his head
while giving her a "you got to be kidding me" smile with a
"tzssss" sound).

JOHN (*long pause*): Oh! You mean…Him??

MARK: Yes, the same one who called me to be a pastor called me to
come to His small space, to His dark place.

LUCY: And you went in…into the cave?

MARK: Yes.

LUCY: Was He there?

MARK: Yes.

LUCY: Where?

MARK: He was sitting on the edge of the flat stone.

LUCY: Did He say anything?

MARK: No. He just patted the edge of the stone, inviting me to sit
next to Him.

LUCY: And did you?

MARK: Yes, of course!

LUCY: And what happened?

MARK: We sat.

JOHN: You sat together in a cave? Weren't you ready to…to

MARK: Freak out?

JOHN: Did you?

MARK: No.

JOHN: But…but weren't you scared?

MARK: Not anymore.

JOHN: How come?

MARK: Because He was beside me! Even now, thinking about His presence…brings me quiet. And then I knew—that He's always been beside me. I felt it in the tomb, and when I thought of that drainage tunnel, He was right there, sitting with me.

JOHN: But how…how do you know that?

MARK: Because I'm in a new movie—with Him! The old movie had me alone in that dark, exploding tunnel. Now Jesus is in there, and nothing can separate me from that love—not even dark drainage tunnels.

LUCY: Even though I walk through the valley of tunnels, I will fear—

MARK (*interrupting*): Lucy! You're an idiot, but very observant.

JOHN: So how do you feel now?

MARK: I feel—I feel… I feel…like dancing! (*He grabs their arms, starts to sway their arms, and sings, "I danced in the morning when the world has begun. And I danced in the moon and the stars…"*)

JOHN AND LUCY (*laughing*): Hey, we're causing a scene! People are looking.

MARK (*He finally stops singing and swaying.*): Oh my, a taste of freedom! But I'm sorry, Lucy.

LUCY: Sorry? Sorry about what?

MARK: You just lost your free breakfast.

LUCY: You're going down into the church crawl space?

MARK: Yep. All by myself!

LUCY: Well, hallelujah! I'll buy *your* breakfast.

JOHN: Well, I'm ready for a bagel, but the conference starts in ten minutes.

LUCY: Well, John, you just have to learn how to pace yourself when you eat.

JOHN AND MARK: Oh please, Lucy! Give us a break!

Discussion Questions

1. What do you think of the way each person's trauma was transformed? What effect did each story have on you? Which transformation had the most impact on you and why? Have you experienced a transformation of your trauma? What is blocking your transformation? Are you trying to transform alone?

2. It seems like the greatest blockage to trauma transformation is asking for help. Why is that? Who and what are your resources for your own transformation? What do you need to surrender in order to access them? What help did Lucy, John, and Mark access and how did they deal with their initial resistance?

3. According to a study of 183 post traumatic police officers, the best predictor of post trauma growth is spirituality. Does that surprise you? What can you conclude, then are the best resources for post-trauma recovery and resiliency?

Possible Responses to DQ

1. All of them had a change in attitude, each in their own specific ways. Transformations do not come all at once, it comes in little specks and baby steps, especially a transformation of recovering from certain trauma. Sometimes people require the presence of others in order to successfully transform. On the other hand, others require solitude instead.

2. Asking for help sometimes feels like the most difficult task one could do, because it could either be embarrassing, scary, and foreign. Sometimes, it can be those three at the same time. People tend to prefer facing things alone because they do not want to burden others, but a helping hand or two can be a significant helping factor in the process of transformation. Just like what all three of them offered to each other that day. Also, Mark, John, and Lucy rose from their fears and doubts, and finally considered the help of the trauma experts.

3. Spirituality tells us to not be afraid. It teaches us to be brave in the face of anything; thus, encouraging us to face trauma. When it comes to the healing transformation from suffering trauma and post-traumatic attitudes, turning to God, the church, the community is the best help that one can get. No man is an island, and even God himself knows this.

CHAPTER 9

The New Movies

Have you ever been a comfort to a friend? Have you ever listened to someone else's problem? Have you ever asked why does your annoying friend or colleague act as such? Have you been considerate in the past, or were you quick to dismiss other people without truly understanding them?

Commentary

For Mark, Lucy, and John, the rubber has hit the road. A transformation has begun. The old movies of "The Exploding Dark Tunnel", "The Deadly Dining Room Table", and "The Failed Sheep Dog" are being transformed through processing and spirituality. The good news is that God is entering the drama and doing what God always does with the wounded. He binds up the broken-hearted, comforts the afflicted, and sets the captives free.

Him who had been traumatized and him who had been raised with power is also the one who can enter into our trauma and raise us with empowerment. With the resurrection of Jesus, all things are made new. Instead of the exploding dark tunnel, Mark is now entering the resurrected tomb. Lucy's deadly dining room table has been transformed to the feast of victory. John's failed sheep dog has become the faithful servant. These are all heroic journeys of redemption, together with each other, under God's name. As a child once said, "It takes at least two to be Jesus!"

The new movies have begun giving the three a new sense of empowerment. It starts their transformation and redemption. They can now watch the old movies, observe their fears and odd behaviors. They can now do these without being held captive in their post-trauma reactions. They now have a choice of which movie they want to view as opposed to reacting to the old movie.

Instead, they can use their past experience and the newly discovered self as a testament to the gifts of God. As they are no longer triggered by their history, they can now share their experience, strength, and hope with others. They can be a living testament that with God, trauma can be overcome. With their experience, they can help many people, especially those who are still stuck in their own trauma movies. Mark, John, and Lucy have become the visible hope of their congregation. They have become a light to those who do not know God, or do not know were they are heading or where to find healing.

Is this not what it meant to follow the Traumatized One? To have life abundantly? Will they not become a trauma-transforming presence? Is healing not God's will?

Reader's Theatre

Act 3, Scene 2: The Conference Resumes

Attendees are making their way to their seats.

SPEAKER: Thank you for reconvening on time. Since most of the counseling sessions were scheduled today and tomorrow, I know that you are working hard on finding the truth—your own truth.

Because you are working hard, we have succeeded... succeeded in providing a safe place, safe enough for you to debrief, to begin to process and learn from your trauma. For these are actually the keys in healing traumatized churches.

The debriefing and processing need to begin shortly after the trauma happened. Else, the trauma would start to be buried in one's mental backyard. Consequently, the longer the time the trauma is in the backyard of memory, the more serious the damage could become. The longer it sits there, the harder it would become for the church to overcome its post-trauma reaction.

AUDIENCE MEMBER: Timing is everything?

SPEAKER: Yes. It is important to have a plan of healing in place. It is crucial to have the plan in the very first month. Or else, the organization will adapt—try to heal itself, to get control and adopt the same methods by which it was traumatized. To unknowingly mimic the same ways that the church was traumatized.AUDIENCE MEMBER: Why would the church do to others (*stops in realization*)…

SPEAKER: What was done unto it?

LUCY: A rat chasing its tail…

SPEAKER: Or a wolverine! (*The audience laughs.*) For example, if the trauma was the abuse of power, look for multiple groups or levels that exhibit abuse of power too. If the abuser used doctrine, ideology, interpretation of Scripture, violations of conscience, or boundary violations, look for people doing the same coercive methods to each other as was done unto them.

MARK: But we are called to be little Christs to one another. So if narcissist leadership abused the congregation…(*pausing and thinking*) are you saying that abuse breeds more narcissists?

SPEAKER: We are all narcissists. Some of us are in remission, and some of us are in relapse.

JOHN: And most don't know the difference! (*The audience responds, "Oh-h-h-h!"*)

SPEAKER: Which one are you? (*Long pause*)

JOHN: I think- I think I'm finally in recovery. I want more recovery. And if God got me here to this conference to begin healing, I know there is a lot more healing to come. (*A few amens from audience*)

SPEAKER: So what is God's will for you?

JOHN: Right now, to be healed. It never registered—even after years of hearing about the miracles of Jesus—that God loves to heal. (*amens from the audience*)

SPEAKER: Heal your church too?

JOHN: Yes.

SPEAKER: But that's not what happened.

JOHN: No, we did not know what to do. Twelve years ago, we were told God's will was for us to move on and forget about it.

SPEAKER: Did it work?

JOHN: No! It changed our whole congregation from being little Christs to one another to a bunch of cranky control freaks—controlling and numb.

AUDIENCE MEMBER: I can't see controlling. How is it that people get so controlling *after* the trauma is over?

SPEAKER: Great question! I need three volunteers for a little experiment.

LUCY (*pausing*): Our group will do it.

JOHN AND MARK: What? Do what? Lucy!

SPEAKER: Lucy the Wolverine bringing two Michigan converts?

LUCY (*as all three make their way to the front*): Not yet, but I'm persistent!

SPEAKER (*responding immediately*): Yes, you are! (*The attendees laugh, and Lucy, John, and Mark finally make their way up.*) I'm glad you made it up here at the wolverine's request. So-o-o, we have Mark, Lucy, and John? (*The audience chuckles.*)

MARK: The significance is not lost on our congregation, either! (*The audience is still chuckling.*)

SPEAKER: Okay, Matthew, Mark, Lucy, and John. (*The audience chuckles.*) Thank you for volunteering. The experiment is one of control. Mark and John, I want you to stand directly behind Lucy and get your arms ready to catch her when she falls backwards.

Lucy: Wo-o-o-w-w! Now wait just a doggone minute. (*The audience laughs.*)
Speaker: You don't think these two big guys will catch you if you fall?
Lucy: Well, yes. I trust them with my life.
Speaker: Good—you trust them. So why hesitate?
Lucy: I don't know. I want to be in (*realization dawning*)…in control! I'll sacrifice faith for control. I'll sacrifice relationships for control. Oh my, I want control! I just lo-o-o-o-ve control! (*The audience laughs.*)
Speaker: And if you fall backwards…
Lucy: I will be out of control.
Speaker: Do you like being out of control?
Lucy: Can't you tell? (*The audience chuckles.*)
Speaker: No one does. When people are traumatized, they feel like they are falling backwards—out of control. So what's a natural reaction to feeling out of control?
John: To get control.
Speaker: Yes. Unprocessed trauma makes people tighten up—get brittle, cranky, and controlling…Preparing for the next shoe to drop, the next trauma to happen. However, to always live life at DEFCON 1, in anticipation of bad things happening again, swings the door open for more control and more trauma. Now if you have a whole group of people trying to be in control, is that still attractive and productive? Just think about it. Would you be attracted to a controlling group?
Lucy: Sure!
Speaker: Okay, Lucy. What in a controlling group of people would be so attractive to you?
Lucy: I'd learn how to be a controller, play the game, imitate the top dog, to be the top dog. (*The audience nervously chuckles.*)
Speaker: And what is that called?
Lucy: Bold sinning! (*The audience has a few amens.*)
Speaker: So how would the controlling group keep control of others?
Audience Member 1: You might as well throw out the gospel.

AUDIENCE MEMBER 2: And throw out people you can't control. All the healthy people—people who will not abandon their brains.

SPEAKER: And how would you get rid of them?

LUCY: Registered mail! (*The audience laughs, but Mark and John look at each other sheepishly.*)

SPEAKER: Thank you, Lucy, Mark, and John. You can go back to your seats. (*As they walk back, he speaks again.*) You were good sports. Let's give them a hand. (*The audience claps.*) Now, any questions? More questions?

MARK (*now seated*): I have one.

SPEAKER: Yes, Mark.

MARK: What you are saying is that the traumatized will try to gain control the same way the traumatizer did.

SPEAKER: Yes. Unless there is healing. Those in fight survival reaction will attempt to gain control in the manner in which they lost it.

MARK: So if people were traumatized, lost control through the abuse of power, they will abuse others with power in order to regain it?

SPEAKER: If they are fighters. The freezers won't; they'll just play dead. And those who flee are gone.

MARK: And if they lost control through neglect or abandonment, they will seek it through being neglectful and abandoning.

SPEAKER: Without healing, they could be neglectful and abandoning.

MARK: And if they lost control through belligerence and dismissiveness, they may try to grab it by being dismissive or belligerent.

SPEAKER: Yes. Unless there is healing, they will continue to do unto others before others can do it unto them, again.

MARK: So when a church is traumatized and has nothing in place to debrief or process the trauma, the church will...will...

SPEAKER: Will eventually get ugly—ugly and nutty—or cold. Or it will just turn inward and have no energy to care about anything but their own personal wants and desires. Personalities and personal agendas take over. The church becomes unsafe and unhealthy. The God of the Bible leaves, as seen by Ezekiel in a chariot with wheels, with the wheels rising above the city.

LUCY: Elvis has left the building! (*The audience has nervous laughter.*)

JOHN (*waiting for audience*): What can be done about the churches that intentionally do not plan for healing?

SPEAKER: Look and pray for the faithful remnant.

JOHN: The what?

SPEAKER: The faithful remnant. The prophets speak of God's faithfulness to the faithful remnant, the people who did not cave in to the unfaithfulness of the dominant culture.

JOHN: But who are the faithful remnant? What do they look like?

SPEAKER: They are easily spotted. They aren't controlling, crankyor numb. They are the ones who have found a way to use their own trauma to become more empathetic with others, more aware of their own shortcomings…more alive, more loving, and more involved in reducing the church's misery rather than creating it. They are the yeast thatmakes the bread rise, the salt of the earth, the leaven of life.

JOHN: But what good are they if the cranky, numbed-out controllers are…well…in control?

SPEAKER: That remnant is that church's last remaining witness that God exists.

MARK (*long pause as audience reacts*): That…that sounds terrible. So what can leaders do?

SPEAKER: True church leadership leads by example.

MARK: What do you mean?

SPEAKER: If you want people to be like the faithful remnant, then do what the faithful remnant does.

MARK: You mean use my own trauma to be…to be more empathetic, more aware, more loving and involved in…in people…in their misery?

SPEAKER: Yes, instead of causing it. Heal your own trauma—don't bury it. Your healing will teach you how to minister to the traumatized. (*long pause*) Sounds simple, doesn't it? (*The audience starts nodding.*) But it's not easy.

MARK: Why is it so hard?

SPEAKER: Look around you, Mark, everyone. Look around this room. You are learning how to pick up your cross and follow the Traumatized One. Have any of you ever done this before? (*He pauses and looks at the attendees.*)No one? Don't you find this…this…odd…that you havenever engaged in conversations about your own traumauntil now—in an organization whose symbol is thetrauma symbol, and whose head is the TraumatizedOne? (*A long pause follows.*) What in the world do youtalk about in church?

JOHN: How much money do we need to keep the lights on?

MARK: How many people do we need to get this project done?

LUCY: Honey, does this dress make me look fat? (*The audience howls.*)

SPEAKER (*He pauses and waits, enjoying the moment.*) I…love…Lucy!

(*The audience applauds Lucy as she yells "yes" and does hervictory dance.*)

SPEAKER (*waiting for everyone to settle.*): So the church is having conversations, but not "*the conversation.*" And are these current conversations helping?

AUDIENCE: No!

SPEAKER: So, if what we are saying and doing is not helping, why do we keep doing it over and over?

MARK: It's all about control. We do it over and over because we were taught to have control. As pastors, we learned the medieval-management style, to centralize power with top-down decision-making. We use doctrines to worship the golden calf of conformity. To control post trauma reactions in traumatized people, we institutionalize trauma's burial and then wonder why we have people fighting, avoiding each other, or even bowing to blank walls.

SPEAKER: That's…that's so hard to hear, isn't it? (*He pauses.*) So, why not do the right thing? Why don't congregations debrief the trauma instead of bury it?

JOHN: We've had no way to talk about it. We had no words nor language— none, until now.

SPEAKER: What's different?

MARK: We now have a language, a framework...to make meaning out of it. And we have a safe place (*He looks around, then at John and Lucy.*) with people who are...who are the yeast, the salt of the earth.

JOHN: For the first time in my life, I'm learning how to be a servant of God.

LUCY: You shall not lord it over others. If you want to be first, be a servant.

SPEAKER: But what if we are not servants of one another? What if we insist on being in control and being in charge? What happens then?

MARK: Then everyone becomes a lord. We become rivals. And every ministry becomes a vassal state, a fiefdom competing for the congregation's attention and dollars—a real political mess and a source of more trauma. Just another rat chasing its tail.

SPEAKER (*breathing deeply*): May God have mercy on us all!

AUDIENCE: Amen!

SPEAKER: But the damage doesn't stop. What happens to the message of the gospel—the love, forgiveness, and grace of the Traumatized One who came to save us?

LUCY: It is replaced by rules, by doctrines, by orthodoxy. We become just like those European Protestants and insist on doing it *the right way—my way with my words—* while bowing to blank walls.

SPEAKER: And what happens to God?

LUCY: God goes in a box. We are left with God-in-the-box, but with all our I's dotted and T's crossed.

SPEAKER: And what word would you use to describe this church, a church that responds to trauma by being controlling, disempowering, and cranky.

JOHN: Stuck!

SPEAKER: Good word. Any others?

AUDIENCE MEMBERS: Unhealthy…sick…dysfunctional family…not safe!

SPEAKER: All good words. So why do we do it? Why do we go to the medieval-management style and centralize all power with top-down decision-making? Any guesses? (*He pauses.*)

LUCY: I got a riddle—a riddle about an alligator.

SPEAKER: An alligator? Not a wolverine? (*The audience chuckles.*)

LUCY: Nope. The riddle begins in a hurricane. A man was swept away into the river when all of a sudden, he saw an alligator swam by. He then jumped on the alligator's back. Now why do you think he jumped on the back of that alligator?

SPEAKER: Anyone here know the answer to the riddle? (*silence*) Okay, Lucy, I give up. Why did the man jump on the back of the alligator?

LUCY: He jumped on the alligator's back because he figured that, compared to him, at least the alligator knew where he was going! (*audience laughter*)

SPEAKER (*waiting*): Lucy, you nailed it. We react to trauma by jumping on alligator backs. It's not smart, it doesn't prolong our lives. But *it's there, it is all that is there.* And so, when you get back in your groups of three, watch out for alligators! (*The audience chuckles.*) But please get into your groups and answer the following questions:

- How do I respond to post-traumatized people?
- Do I get more controlling, more empathetic, more patient, more gracious?
- Do I tolerate the traumatized or insist they put on a happy face?

Please discuss these questions.

(*Both Mark and John look at each other, shake their heads, and sigh.*)

LUCY (*noticing the reactions of both Mark and John*): Hey, what's up? Did I do something wrong? You both look like you came out of an explosion.

JOHN: Lucy, we have a confession to make.

MARK: This happened before you accepted the call to the church.

LUCY: Oh, okay. What's up?

MARK: I fired the altar guild.

LUCY: You did what?

MARK :I fired the altar guild.

LUCY (*Shocked, she looks at him and pauses.*): By registered mail?

MARK (*pausing*): No, I was sneakier. Just before you accepted the call, I just—just…cleaned house. They were so controlling, backing everyone into a corner with their heat-seeking blame missiles. I felt so…so trapped. So I fired them.

JOHN: And I helped.

LUCY: You did what?

JOHN: I helped to fire them. They were so…so dismissive of anyone who questioned or used their brains…

MARK:… And didn't park their brains and hearts outside.

JOHN: It was ugly. Right after the former pastor finally left, they volunteered to take over both the worship and music tasks. At first, everyone was grateful because we were all so…so devastated. But then everything had to go through them, the music, the service, even the scheduling. They had total control of Sunday morning.

MARK: That committee…it just wasn't safe or hospitable to anyone… especially for people with a new idea. They drove everyone else away…everyone who did not bend to their control.

JOHN: Well, they even recruited those they could control,giving the new people on the committee leadership positions despite incompetence. Back then, the only thing that mattered was that they got their own way, that they had control. So, it didn't matter if the person did not know anything. In fact, they wanted only figure heads to manipulate and bend to their ways.

LUCY: Controlling, demanding, dismissive, wanted their own way... So, they did to the church what you did to your family, John. They also mimicked the abusive pastor.

JOHN: Yeah. (*He pauses.*) We all did. And I am so sorry. They were on the old pastor's radar. He targeted them. He was unmerciful in his public ridicule. He humiliated them. He made them the butt of his jokes. And so I did to them what they were doing to everyone else. I supported the firing.

LUCY: But how? How could you fire them...from a church?

MARK: Well, we didn't exactly fire them. We did the old end-around.

LUCY: O-oh-h-h. So you did the old "organizational restructuring" deal?

MARK: Yeah. We divided up the committee and then just outsourced their most visible functions to other committees—just a damage control...that's all...just doing damage control.

LUCY: They were fired and they didn't know it.

MARK: We had to do something. It was a total impediment for worship. It was scandalous—the nutty decision-making and the chaos it created. But I wish I knew *then*...

JOHN: Yeah, so do I, Mark. So do I.

MARK: I feel bad. What a wasted opportunity for healing! But instead, I took care of it. I was in charge, in control. They backed me into a small space, and I reacted. I used the old standby, the medieval-management style top-down decision-making.

JOHN: And I was your vassal.

LUCY: But there's no way both of you could have known. You both had no idea what questions to ask. And if you had asked the right ones, how could you have made sense out of it? You had no words or framework to understand anything.

JOHN (*pausing, sighing*): Post-trauma reaction.

MARK: (*mimicking the sigh*): Post-trauma codependency, trying to control the controllers.

LUCY: What we do to the poor sheep!

JOHN: Such a ba-a-a-ad idea!

LUCY: Hey, watch it. I'm the comedian!

MARK: Not anymore. Move over, Lucy. Old Mister Intensity has his humor back!
JOHN: Hey, you guys, I'm tryin', really tryin'!
LUCY: And doin' just fine, John. You're doin' just fine.

Discussion Questions

1. Lucy realized her love of being in control. Is she unique, or is there a deep human attraction to control? What does it take to surrender control? Even though we have little control in this life, what is so attractive about control that would cause us to do anything to have it on our hands? What would you be willing to do to get control? How does this attraction to control affect the way people talk to each other, how they organize, and the fulfillment of the organization's mission? How did the snake use the allure of control in the Garden of Eden?

2. God's faithful remnant resists controlling other people, places, and things. They are not motivated by control, but powered by empathy to others' trauma and their desire to becoming involved. They are safe to talk to because they meet people in their pain and suffering without judgement. Their mission is to heal, as Jesus did, and in Jesus' name. How do you know whether or not you are a faithful remnant?

3. John and Mark suddenly realized how they attempted to control rather than heal the church by "firing the altar guild." What changes made them suddenly realize their participation in trauma's burial? Have you ever done what they did in order to "just move on?" Is this fulfilling our mission to heal the sick, raise the dead, and comfort the afflicted?

Possible Responses to DQ

1. All humans love being in control. This is because we inherently like to experience having the power to manage ourselves without anyone else telling us what to do. It also makes us feel powerful and invulnerable. However, too much need for control is dangerous, too. Without boundaries, those who are in control are very likely to abuse their power, and the people under them.

2. You will know if you are a faithful remnant simply by how you respond to other people or other communities. If you have the urge to control and lead organizations without accepting help, guidance, or suggestions, you are not a member. However, if you choose to be one with the people, to understand and heal like what Jesus did, then you are definitely a faithful remnant.

3. They were asked by the speaker about how did they respond to traumatized people. Upon realization, they remembered how they indirectly fired the controlling guild in their church.

    Back then, the guild was controlling the Sunday morning of their church. Both Mark and John felt like they were losing control and instead were being controlled. This prompted them to respond, to grab the reigns and do what had been done to them. This is not what God taught us. He had taught us to surrender and be compassionate to one another. Become bearers of comfort to each other, not induce fear and take control.

CHAPTER 10

No More Wasted Opportunities

*What is the purpose of "life lessons?" What is their importance?
As someone who has learned before—personally or spiritually,
were you able to extend such learnings to others? Were you
able to touch other people's lives the same way that yours was
touched? If so, what did you feel after doing that act of kindness?
And if you haven't done it yet, what are the impediments?*

Commentary

John and Mark are now using their newly discovered self-knowledge
to look at their own activities, how they reacted and unknowingly
participated in trauma's burial. They saw a hotspot, a traumatized
committee that imitated the controlling, unilateral decision-making of the former sheep-beating leadership. Without the knowledge
about trauma healing, the committee just buried their trauma. It then
gained control by beating others as they had been beaten. Anyone
who would go against their personal agendas were mistreated too,
in the name of Jesus! When Mark became the pastor of the church,
he did not do any trauma history. Back then, he had no idea of the
extent of the damage. Even worse, he didn't know how to address the
damage. He simply did not know what he was doing, how to frame
what the committee was doing, and how to heal, frame, or manage it.

As a trained pastor, Mark knew the tricks of top-down unilateral decision-making and how to indirectly neutralize problems through reorganization. He was remorseful. But without a trauma history, relevant questions would not be asked and a positive healing plan would not be created. Even alternative options would not be considered. As a result, he resorted to fixing the problem the best way he knew how. Fixing it institutionally by burying it.

And so, Mark divided and conquered. He outsourced the problem. Without a history, language, or framework, relevant questions weren't asked, and no alternative options were generated. Can you imagine how many ministries have resorted to the same institutional-administrative solutions to take control of other people's post-traumatic reactions? Can you imagine how many trauma healing opportunities were waisted? Can this basic trauma education be what church leaderships really need?

Reader's Theatre

Act 3, Scene 3: The Choices for Leadership

SPEAKER: Thank you for your participation. Now please return to your seats. (*He shuffles back to the podium.*) Okay, thank you for your prompt return.

Are you ready for the last church-trauma story for today? Okay, as we just demonstrated, trauma causes us to lose our balance, to lose control. It feels like we are falling backwards. And just like falling backwards, we grab onto something—anything—for control.

Congregations have the same post trauma reaction—to grab onto anything for control. Following trauma, congregations experience reeling and panicking. Imagine a swimmer who experienced cramps in the water. All of the sudden, he loses control. Because of his dire need of control, to get hold of himself and to prevent him from drowning, the swimmer may grab onto the throat of the lifeguard. And so do the congregations. After trauma, they are in the same desperate need for control. As a result, they may try to get hold of the throat of anyone who is within arms reach.

In post-trauma reaction, congregations grab onto many different things for control—people, places, and even alligators! (*The audience chuckles.*) Sometimes congregations grab onto the control promised by the centralization of power, employing a tight structure of organizational top-down decision-making. With this type of repressive regime, they believe they already gain control, when in fact, they are actually creating more trauma and more chaos.

Congregations also grab onto control by calling out other persons who are in control, even if that control is for the better. Congregations may put a grip on someone who is "keeping a tight rein on things, getting things done, tying up the loose ends, and steering the community in the right direction." Unfortunately, the leadership of such congregations are, more often than not, the people who are in love with control. They love being in control and even resort to abusing power to get more of it. They never even see the people they wound, only the false sense of security of having more power.

And in some cases, there are congregations who, like Scarlett, shake their fists at the Southern sky and vow, "I'll never be traumatized again!" And so they choose a pastor whom they feel *they* can control.

There was once a traumatized congregation who chose a pastor whom they felt they could control. The pastor lacked leadership and relational skills, and the sermons—they are surely a cure for insomnia. So how in the world did the call committee even consider such a person?

AUDIENCE MEMBER: They must have had a previous pastor who was out of control.

SPEAKER: Yes. Out of control, lacking personal boundaries.

LUCY: So the previous pastor loved the sheep *too much!*

SPEAKER (*as the audience oohs*): Well, you could put it that way. He was charming, with relational and communication skills. His charm charmed the congregation—right into boundary violations. And the church was traumatized that their pastor would take advantage of them. Therefore, the call committee was put on notice—no more of that kind. And so, the call committee called someone who couldn't lead, couldn't talk… who was not at all charming.

AUDIENCE MEMBER: Wisdom at work! (*The audience groans.*)

SPEAKER: Actually, post-trauma reaction at work. However, a couple of years later, the church decided to call an assistant pastor. So another call committee was put in place, but this call committee was sick and tired of the lack of leadership. And so they looked for someone who "could take charge" and "get control of this congregation".

AUDIENCE (*reacting*): Oh no!

SPEAKER: Oh yes! And so the call committee called a controlling assistant pastor, attempting to balance the skills challenged senior pastor. (*Audience groans, "Oh no, I can't believe it!"*)

Do you see the potential for fireworks? (*The audience replies affirmatively.*) One had leadership skills, but no authority. The other had authority, but no leadership skills. (Audience groans, "What a disaster!")

Now, how many trauma cycles need to run before the damage is beyond repair and the church becomes deadly? And yet, somehow, the dots never get connected. The terror-driven pursuit of control pushes us to do the familiar, to do the same thing over and over. And yet we still expect different results?Many of you come from churches stuck in repetitive post-trauma cycles. And so, your afternoon assignment from now until late afternoon, is to develop an initial plan of intervention. So, when you get back to your councils, congregations, Bible studies, fellowship groups, and Sunday schools, and people ask you, "Why did you go there?" You can answer them, "To get a plan."

Take care, and see you later.

Act 3, Scene 4: The Plan

MARK: Well, thanks to John, we already know the church's trauma history.

LUCY: And we have had firsthand experiences of being fighters, fliers, and freezers.

JOHN: And so on to the plan! Let's get going!

MARK: It's so frustrating! This should have been done twelve years ago. What if we can't afford the resources? What if we can't get any buy-in from the congregation? What if we can't—

LUCY (*interrupting*): Mark, are you trapping yourself in a dark place?

MARK (*long pause*): Yes. Oh, I mean no…Your right. Thank you, Lucy.

LUCY: No problemo!

JOHN: But Mark, that "what iffing" you just did is probably how some will react to us when we go home.

(*There is a long pause followed by simultaneous, obvious sighs.*)

LUCY: So-o-o, what's the plan?

JOHN: Do we even know what to call the plan?

MARK: How about "A Corrective Action Plan"?

LUCY: Naw, too sterile.

JOHN: Well, what are we really trying to do?

MARK: To do for the congregation what we've experienced here.

JOHN: And what was that?

MARK: Life—we've been given some life.

JOHN: Well, it's sure eye opening.

LUCY: It gave me the good ne-e-ews…without noo-oo-se!

(*Both John and Mark look at Lucy and groan. Lucy smiles back, batting her eyes. They shake their heads.*)

MARK: Well, the plan has to be uplifting, give life, and…good ne-e-ews!

LUCY: Now you've got it!

JOHN: Now that you've got it, what would we call it?

LUCY: Sounds like...hmmm, something like resurrection!

MARK: "A Plan of Resurrection..."

LUCY: How about "A Celebration of Resurrection?"

JOHN (*pausing*): Wait, are we going to celebrate the trauma from twelve years ago?

MARK: No, not the trauma, but the life that God creates from it! If God took the trauma of the cross and turned that mess into a gift, then surely God can take *any* trauma and transform it into giving new life.

LUCY: Definitely! The gifts that we have been given...

MARK: ...Gifts we finally saw when we faced our traumas.

JOHN (*pausing*): Huh. I can get on board with that. So what's the plan?

MARK: We tell them the truth.

JOHN: Which truth?

LUCY: Our own truth! The truth we have been given and how it's affected us and our relationship with God.

MARK: And our own relationships, too. (*smiling and looking at John and Lucy*)

JOHN (*pausing*): Hm-m-m-m. "The Truth About Trauma"—has a ring, doesn't it? "The Truth...About Trauma"

MARK: And another truth...the truth about God.

LUCY: The God whose trauma saves us.

MARK: Putting the cross and trauma back together!

JOHN: I get it. Tell them the truth, the whole truth...

LUCY: And nothing but the truth!

JOHN: But how would we get them get their truth?

MARK: The same way we got at ours. First, we have to make them feel safe. Then, we teach them...teach them about the importance of the words...the language. And finally, develop a structure with them, and guide them along the way. How does that sound?

JOHN: Sounds effective! But where and how do we begin?

LUCY: (*thinking*) How about we begin with our own truth, our own experience, strength, and hope. Aha! We should start the conversation by example.

MARK: We can call it "Healing Trauma" groups.

JOHN: Sounds good. And then what?

MARK: We give to them what we were given. We provide a language, a framework, and a structure—the same things. And they'll do what we did.

JOHN: And what was that exactly?

MARK: They'll give themselves to each other...

LUCY: ...As Jesus gave Himself to us.

JOHN (*pausing*): But how will they do that?

MARK: By the power of three! Just put them in groups of three.

JOHN: The listener, the speaker, and the observer?

MARK AND LUCY: Definitely, yes!

LUCY: "Where two or three are gathered together in My name..."

JOHN: Okay, then what?

MARK: Give them the structure like we were given, questions they can use to tell their own experience, strength, and hope.

LUCY: Like, "When you think of a personal trauma, what pictures do you see, and how do you feel about those pictures today?"

MARK: And, "When you think of what happened, does it feel like you are watching a rerun, or does it feel like it's still happening, like you're still in the movie?"

LUCY: And, "What have you said to yourself about being in a trauma movie?"

MARK: And then, "What talents and gifts have you discovered about yourself, as a result of making it through the trauma?"

LUCY: And, "How has this trauma changed you and your relationship to God and others?"

MARK: And lastly, "Who supported you in helping you with the trauma and How can you use your experience, strength, and hope to help others face their life traumas?"

JOHN: Great! This is awesome! I'm so excited! But where do we begin?

LUCY AND MARK (*They look at each other and then at John; then they speak simultaneously*): The church council!

JOHN (*looking up, rolling eyes*): Are you kidding me?

LUCY: But John, don't you just lo-o-o-ove those council meetings?

MARK: And all the woulda-coulda-shouldas…

LUCY: And crabby "what iffing" and the "ain't gots"?

JOHN (*long pause, then speaks nonchalantly*): No.

(*Mark and Lucy laugh.*)

LUCY: Aw, c'mon John! Where's your sense of adventure?

JOHN: I'm a vet—saw the world *twice*.

MARK (*long pause*): John, what's holding you back?

JOHN: I—I just don't…well (*sudden realization*), a couple of "shouldas", but only one "what if."

LUCY: Caught yourself, didn't you?

JOHN: Sure did!

MARK: Are you in?

JOHN: I'm in!

LUCY: So am I!

MARK (*putting out his fist*): All for one…

LUCY, MARK, AND JOHN (*their fists joining*): And one for all!

LUCY: Let's get a quick bite…eh-h-h…I mean, let's go to lunch.

JOHN: Caught yourself, too huh?

LUCY: Sure did. Let's eat—all together!

Discussion Questions
(Act 3, Scene 3)

1. When calling a pastor, what characteristics are you looking for? Following a traumatic experience, what would color your vision in your decision making process? Do you think an implementation of a healing plan for the congregation would affect their choice of pastor? How would it affect your vision if you would be on the call committee?

2. Churches can either respond and develop plans for healing the trauma, or, continue doing the same things that do

not work. And so, churches have the freedom to just keep burying it, saying, "we are determined to just move on.". What do you make of the church who called a senior pastor they could control, but an assistant pastor to lead? What would you do if you were a member of that church?

Possible Responses to DQ

1. The characteristics one should be looking for are those that reflect what God intended for us to have. Knowledgeable and wise compassion, kindness, empathy, and rationality. It's important to remember what caused the trauma to surface, to respond in healthy ways, and to focus on a consistent healing regimen and protocol that the pastor can follow and lead through.
2. Controlling and leading are two very different things. But the common denominator between the two is that they take the form of authority, though executed in different ways. To control is to show dominance, but showing dominance and control is like using a bar of soap: The more you use it, the less you have. Only in crisis situations and emergencies, control may be needed.
3. However, to lead is to gain authority through empathy, which is what congregations need most of the time. Empathy provides a safe place to heal, but also, a way to talk to the congregation so that what the pastor said is taken to heart and seriously considered and prayed over. Jesus used his control only once – to drive out the money changers in the temple. So, what was he doing the rest of the time? Showing compassion to people by speaking the good news, listening to their wounds, and healing them". Jesus lived his life as the servant king. Perhaps the church should do likewise?

Discussion Questions
(Act 3, Scene 4)

1. If you were to develop a healing plan for your congregation, would your goals be:

   - make a safe space for people to talk,
   - provide education to give people language and frameworks to make meaning out of their trauma, and
   - establish an ongoing structure of continuing care and resources?

   How would you begin that conversation and who would be key to the process? What would that plan look like and how would you implement it?

2. What do you make of the following group discussion questions to illicit people to share their experience strength and hope:

   - When you think of personal trauma, what pictures do you see, what feelings arise, and what body sensations do you experience?
   - When you think of what happened, does it feel like you are back experiencing it, or, is it more like watching a re-run on TV?
   - What have you said to yourself about yourself as a result of the trauma?
   - What talents, gifts, and strengths have you discovered about yourself from living through the traumatic experience?
   - How has the experience of this trauma changed you and your relationship to God and others?
   - How can you use your experience, strength, and hope to help others face their life traumas?

Possible Responses to DQ

1. This is the most effective set of goals that could possibly aid the development and growth of healing within a congregation. Beginning the conversation should be comfortable, through easing the people into a lighthearted conversation on their personal experiences and sharing one from your own, and looking back to God as the bearer of healing from trauma should be the most critical factor in this plan.
2. This immerses the people involved in an easy and comfortable way. It is not aggressive, it is not overly-provoking, it does not intrude, but it invites participation in a safe and healthy way. It provokes the right amount of thought that should be present among the members of the congregation, and these questions do that perfectly. Facing your fears is not an abrupt action, it is a process that could take minutes, days, weeks, months, and sometimes years.

CHAPTER 11:

The Road Map

It is said that, "It takes a great man to give sound advice tactfully, but a greater to accept it graciously." What would you do if you've given a sound advice to a person whom you thought was in a dire need, and found out that your advice wasn't taken? Would you be hurt and let the person suffer on his own? Or would you be firm and committed to walk by his or her side to look deeper into the real problems?

Commentary

Mark, Lucy, and John were developing their plan to make the congregation trauma resilient. By definition, resiliency is the ability to bounce back from trauma no matter how painful it is. Congregations who have the words, language framework, organizational structure, and commitment to healing trauma are the ones ready to follow the Traumatized One.

When everything's ready and the plan has already been laid, the only missing piece is the living testaments. The congregation needs a personal witness, a person who can testify to the goodness of God, and God's provision to heal. And knowing wholeheartedly what the conference have done to them, Mark, Lucy, and John are more than willing to be their church's living new testaments.

All three are willing to give personal testimony of their healing journey with God. They have powerful stories of salvation, moments of clarity, and unimagined gifts from God. They already have a five-question structure to assist people in identifying trauma, as well as to lift up God's gifts. It is a new language, a new framework—a trauma framework to empower meaningful sharing, faith, and resiliency.

As they put flesh on the rest of their resurrection-celebration plan, they come up with the need to define the following—their plan's goals, vision, methods, measurements, and the specific steps.

To make their plan more effective, the three decided to follow a plan similar to this:

GOAL: Congregational life, growth, and resiliency through facing and mulching trauma into wisdom.

VISION: Educating the congregation by providing trauma-language frameworks, trauma theology, and trauma mission.

METHODS: Personal-trauma-healing testimonies, sermons, retreats, leadership training, drama, small healing group, trauma-healing services, discussions of the healing-trauma stories of the Bible, etc.

MEASUREMENTS: Increased congregational life, energy, and empathy as measured by:

Time spent in fellowship, worship, and outreach. Formulation of healing groups.

Formulation of trauma-ministry task force.

Increased participation in leadership training, Sunday school discussion, Bible study groups, etc.

SPECIFIC STEPS FOR BOTH CLERGY AND LAY LEADERSHIP: A commitment from the leadership to become trauma educated, to do a thorough personal-trauma history, and then seek assistance in healing their personal trauma. Then use those personal-trauma gifts to lead, educate, heal, and make the congregation more trauma resilient.

A commitment from the leadership to provide the educational and healing structures for congregations to safely examine personal trauma. This is to ensure that trauma is acknowledged and healed, not controlled, hidden, or buried.

A commitment from the leadership to use the authority of the Traumatized One to be a servant of trauma survivors by normalizing, validating, and connecting them to congregational life and health.

A commitment from the leadership to celebrate trauma's redemption and gifts of being transformed from trauma survivors to being trauma thrivers.

So, with all the plan in place, would you want to be a member of such church? Should we name it as "The Task Force of The Traumatized One?"

Reader's Theatre

Act 3, Scene 5: Whose Fool Are We?

SPEAKER: This afternoon it was obvious how hard you were all working on your healing plans for your congregations. Every plan seemed to fit your situations. You all had enthusiasm. Does anyone know what *enthusiasm* means?

AUDIENCE MEMBER: It comes from *en theos*, "to be filled with God".

SPEAKER: And so are all of you! So what do you expect from your congregations when you present your healing plans? What do you think will they do? What will happen when you arrive at the church doors?

LUCY: Palm Sunday! (*The audience laughs.*)

SPEAKER (*waiting*): With or without donkeys? (*The audience chuckles.*)

LUCY (*waiting*): We'll find an ass or two. (The audience reacts with "Who-o-o-ah!")

SPEAKER (*pausing for audience reaction*): Lucy, what animal is more dangerous than a wolverine?

LUCY: There ain't no such animal! (*The audience chuckles.*)

SPEAKER: Yes, there is. The animal more dangerous than a wolverine is a *wounded* wolverine.

LUCY (*pausing*): Okay, but what's your point?

SPEAKER: My point is this. You are taking your healing plan into a church where sheep got beat. They got beat up really really bad. But they survived by burying their trauma and then centralized all power in top-down decision-making to ensure its continued burial. So what do you expect will happen when they start thinking and feeling about what's been buried in the church's backyard... For a very long time? Who will they blame when the trauma once again resurfaces? (*There is dead silence, a long pause.*)

So you're going home with the first gifts of healing... carrying some knowledge and personal experience, and a healing plan on the other hand. Now how do you approach the beaten sheep? How would you approach their wounds?

LUCY: With fear and trembling.

SPEAKER: Isn't fear and trembling what you brought to this conference in the first place?

MARK: Yeah. I wanted to leave.

JOHN: I tried to leave, but Lucy threatened to nail my other foot to the floor! (*The audience chuckles.*)

SPEAKER: So Lucy, when you go back to the church, do you have enough nails for everybody's feet? (*The audience snickers.*)

LUCY: No more nails! I just need...myself.

SPEAKER: Interesting. Is that all?

LUCY: Yeah. I just have to "bring it"—just myself, and tell the truth, my own truth.

SPEAKER: And what truth is that?

LUCY: My truth is this. I was scared to death, terrified of what was buried. I wanted to run but thankfully, I didn't.

SPEAKER: What were the nails that held you back?

LUCY: Just one nail. A few months ago, I began looking in the mirror and said to my reflection, "I can't do this, can't be a pastor for another twenty years. Something has to change."

SPEAKER: And has anything changed?

LUCY: Yes, absolutely! I'm on a different path now. A different road… freedom's road. Not the road to the burial sites… No, that road doesn't exist anymore. Not now and no more. I'm awake!

SPEAKER: Not afraid?

LUCY: Oh, I'm afraid, but not from the backyard.

SPEAKER: So where's your fear?

LUCY: I'm scared about the "gotta do" list, that's all.

SPEAKER: The "gotta do" list?

LUCY: Yeah. I gotta trust God…trust God and (*looks at John and Mark*)…and…gotta trust these two guys here. Gotta give up control. Gotta be honest, transparent, and share my journey, and gotta know that not everyone will understand.

SPEAKER: So there's a cost to all those "gottas," to being real and faithful. Have you counted the cost?

LUCY (*in preacher cadence, standing*): I want to be a witness of the resurrection!(*The audience responds with "amens" during her speaking.*) I'm not going home the same way I came. I'm going back a different way! (*The audience amens.*) I won't go back, back to what I've always done, because it puts me down—down in the basement! (*The audience amens, and Lucy crescendos.*) I was down in the basement, but no more. I'm not going back down—down to that old basement—but up—up to the dining room table! I've been lifted up (*more amens*), lifted up and brought to dine at the feast—the feast of victory! (*more amens*)

(*Lucy speaks more softly but crescendos at the end.*) I'm no longer just a pastor, but a witness, a witness to God's healing inside of me. (*more amens*) I am a witness of God's power to take on anything and make it all anew. (*louder amens*) I am a witness to the resurrection (*louder amens*), to the resurrection of the body, the body of Christ. Up from the grave, she rises again! (*The audience stands, applauding.*)

SPEAKER (*pausing for the audience to be seated*): So you are about to take a journey you have never made…to a land you've never seen…to be blessed by a God who doesn't give out maps?

173

LUCY (*pausing*): Sounds like I'm Abraham. Well (*looking at her chest*)...closer to Sarah! (*The audience laughs.*)

SPEAKER: And some will fight you, others will flee from you, and a whole bunch of people will just look at you like deer in headlights. Anyone else have any thoughts on this? Yes? Questions? (*The speaker's voice fades into the background.*)

MARK (*whispering*): Lucy, that was so honest, so brave—wow!

JOHN: You had me at "no more nails!"

LUCY (*pausing and looking at both*): What are you talking about?

MARK: You just testified to this group in the same way all of us should do back at the church!

JOHN: You gave everyone permission to be real, to tell the truth—the whole truth. And they loved you.

MARK: Your faith...your witness! That's all we need. Our honesty and hope from our own struggles—we just need to open up...

JOHN: Yes, our minds and hearts!

LUCY (*pausing, smiling*): So, you both love me, huh?

MARK: Yes! (*He pauses, realization dawning.*) Oh, so...so you want us to...to say it?

LUCY: Of course!

JOHN: Can't talk you out of it?

LUCY: Just try!

JOHN (*looking around*): Right here? Right Now?

LUCY: Yep.

MARK: Okay, you win.

LUCY: Always do. C'mon, guys, say it together. A one, a two, a three...

MARK AND JOHN (*looking at each other, looking at Lucy, whispering loudly*): I...love...Lucy!

LUCY (*whispering, giving a thumbs-up*): Yes!

SPEAKER: Okay. Again, great questions. Thank you. I have one last story before we wrap up. This story is about a doctor who practiced medicine before Louis Pasteur discovered germ theory. Dr. Sandmel did not know about germs, but he did pay attention to a majority of birthing mothers dying of infection in the hospital just after the doctors had delivered their babies.

However, when mothers had children delivered by midwives, hardly any of them were infected, let alone died. He observed that the only difference between the actions of the doctors and midwives was that the midwives washed their hands before delivery. His hunch was that the hand washing had something to do with most of the women living past childbirth.

His hunch led him to confront the doctors with his observations. Initially, Sandmel convinced the reluctant doctors to wash their hands before delivering the babies. Complaining, they washed their hands, and the result was that few mothers died.

Now what do you think the medical society did for Dr. Sandmel's great work in saving the lives of all those birthing mothers?

LUCY: Nobel Prize! (*The audience chuckles.*)

SPEAKER: Well, that's a tad bit early. But no, they did not praise, honor, or celebrate his work. Nor did they celebrate the lives of the women saved. In fact, all the doctors went back to their normal child-delivery routine, the *not*-washing-their-hands routine! And as expected, mothers were infected just like before, and they died.

AUDIENCE (*reacting*): That's outrageous! Why?.... Why did they not wash their hands?!

SPEAKER: Now why did they go back to not washing their hands, despite the research provided by Dr. Sandmel? (*long pause*)

JOHN: They...they just didn't want to wash their hands.

SPEAKER: Yes! Despite all the mothers who were saved, they just didn't want to. (*long pause*) Why? What would they have to give up if they continued to wash their hands?

JOHN: Control! They would have to give up control!

SPEAKER: Is it easy, to give up control? AUDIENCE: No!

SPEAKER: How come?

LUCY: It's just easier to let the mothers die than to give up control.

SPEAKER (*long pause, dead silence*): Sounds dangerous to those challenging the controllers. (*He pauses.*)

MARK: Better that one man die than the whole nation perish. (*There is a frozen, dead silence and long pause.*) SPEAKER: Better that all die than for me to lose control. (*There is another frozen, long, dead silence.*) AUDIENCE MEMBER: So what happened to Dr. Sandmel?

SPEAKER: He died in an insane asylum, placed there by the medical society.

(*There is a long pause while the audience reacts with shock and disgust.*) He died of the same disease he tried to stop the mothers from getting. (*The audience reacts more loudly.*) He died expecting that the other doctors would be more logical, more compassionate, but they were numb to both logic and compassion.

He died because his own compassion and curiosity led

Him to speak the truth to the belligerent and controlling medical society.

JOHN (*long pause*): Are you saying that when we return home, we need to lose any...any positive expectations?

SPEAKER: No. I'm saying that you need to lose *all expectations!* If you want people to participate and carry with them their worst traumas hidden in the backyard, then be sure to pay attention and walk beside them. Lead with a compassionate and a curious heart. They need you with them, not against them. You should not fight with them and insist how they *should* feel. You should not flee from them simply because they tell you how they feel or because they're frozen and unable to speak. During those moments, all they need is the feeling of safety. And you should be there to give them such assurance.

JOHN (*pausing*): Just walk with them...

SPEAKER: Yes.

JOHN: Because they need your company...

SPEAKER: Yes.

JOHN: And let God do the healing.

SPEAKER: Yes. You only need to be a witness to their pain and to the God who enters their pain.

JOHN: And that's called...grace?

SPEAKER: Yes, and it's all we need.

AUDIENCE MEMBER: But where do we begin?

SPEAKER: In the Garden of Gethsemane. Pray, "Not my but Thy will be done." Pray and then grab onto the cross and don't let go. And then get back up! Safe support from the faithful remnant who has your back, people who aren't afraid to walk with you in your own trauma backyard. And stick with your plan, your plan of healing for the congregation. Questions?

AUDIENCE MEMBER: You've given the worst-case scenario with Dr. Sandmel. What's the—

LUCY (*interrupting*): I have another riddle!

SPEAKER (*pausing*): Okay, Lucy. Another alligator? (*The audience chuckles.*)

LUCY: No—a pig! (*The audience chuckles.*)

SPEAKER: A pig? Your new riddle is about a pig?

LUCY: Absolutely!

SPEAKER: You all want to hear about Lucy's pig? AUDIENCE: Go for it. Let's hear it! Yeah! SPEAKER: Okay, Lucy. Share your pig.

LUCY: Okay. There was once a man who was driving down the road when all of a sudden, just ahead of him, another car came around the corner, swerving back and forth in both lanes, out of control. And just when they were about to collide, the out-of-control car righted itself, and the driver screamed at the man, "Pig!" Well, the man took great offense at this crazy driver calling him a name, so he screamed back, "Hog!" and kept driving around the corner. So-o-o-o...guess what happened when the driver went around the corner?

SPEAKER: I have no idea.

LUCY: Well (*She starts to laugh.*)...he went right around the corner (she starts to snort) ...and ran over a pig! (*She pauses, and then the audience howls.*)

SPEAKER (*waiting for audience*): There is a moral to that story...

LUCY: Of course! The moral is if you want to bring home the bacon— all together now...

AUDIENCE: Don't run over the pig! (*laughter*)

SPEAKER (*waiting for the audience*): There is a deeper moral to that story, isn't there, Lucy?

LUCY: Yeah. If we go back to our congregations, and even if our plan do work, to some people, we will still look like the crazy driver, screaming loudly, "Pig!"

SPEAKER: And the congregation won't just be calling you names, will they?

LUCY: No. It could get costly—very costly.

SPEAKER: Laying your life down for the sheep?

LUCY: A good shepherd.

(*There is a long silence.*)

AUDIENCE MEMBER: So what's the best-case scenario? (*The audience has nervous laughter.*)

SPEAKER: You all want the best-case scenario for those who warn of the pig in the road?

AUDIENCE: Yes, tell us! ... What do we do?

SPEAKER: The best-case scenario is that you become the court jester, the fool in the king's court.

AUDIENCE (*reacting*): What? What do you mean?... How can we...?

SPEAKER: The king's fool is the only one who can tell the truth to the king, to the controllers, and not get his head chopped off.

AUDIENCE (*reacting*): But how?... What can we say?... Or do?

SPEAKER: Use yourselves and your own struggles to tell the truth. Poke fun at your own backyard burials. Laugh at yourselves. But whatever you do, don't take yourselves seriously.

That opens the door for power struggles with controllers, who *always* take themselves seriously. Tell your own experience, strength, and hope with humility and humor, and you will become a fool as opposed to a dead doctor!

JOHN: So we become fools—fools for Christ's sake.

SPEAKER: A fool for Christ—and no one else.

LUCY (after long pause): I can live with that—called to be Christ's fool!

178

SPEAKER: That's the key—*to live!* To be a *living* witness…to stay alive in your calling…is all you need to do. (*a few amens from the audience*)

Not as enthusiastic? Good. That's a piece of truth that needs a lot more chewing. Take your time. This afternoon you can continue to meet with the trauma experts and also work on your return-home plans. Then this evening, for the last part of the conference, we will close the convention in the worship area. I want to show you some windows—picture windows!

Discussion Questions

1. If trauma is buried, it is hurting your church's mission, vision, outreach, stewardship and leadership choices. What, then, is the natural reaction of those who are called to heal when beginning to engage in the healing process? Is the result any different than the pain of re-setting a broken leg from its normal position? How does church leadership respond to those who want to keep the trauma buried regardless of the negative effects of its continued burial has on the church? What does the leadership need to prepare for so that Dr. Sandmel's history is not repeated? What do you make of the role of "Christ's Fool?" Are you ready to warn people and scream, "PIG!?"

2. Jesus said, "physician, heal thyself." Therefore, what is the first step church leadership needs to do in order to bring healing to the church? What will it take and what needs to be surrendered for self healing to occur?

Possible Responses to DQ

1. The first and natural reaction of the people who have buried trauma is to bury themselves as well, hiding in the shadows, away from their feelings, experiences, and emo-

tions. However, for a person in the process of healing, they slowly step away from the darkness, taking baby steps or big leaps, into the light and further into the rays of brightness. Churches need to be ready for those who will reject the healing and stick to what they know, rather than choosing to step out of their supposed "comfort" zones. In this case, we have to be ready at all times to provide the truth, love, and reassurance to everyone in the community and the congregation.

2. Reassurance and locating the right area to place trust is what leaders of congregations should be doing. It takes accountability, courage, acceptance, and willingness to change in order to properly initiate the development of self-growth and healing.

CHAPTER 12:

Snakes and Stained Glass

As you read this book, what are the greatest fears, embarrassment, anxiety, or frustration that came to your mind? After finishing the first eleven chapters, have you mustered the courage to face your very own trauma? When you see them directly in your face, would you run and cry? Or would you ask God for the courage to be decided, facing your trauma and transforming it to life-long lessons?

Commentary

Expectations are resentments waiting to be born. The scene asked us, "What do you expect from the wounded? What do you expect will happen when introducing trauma conversations to the congregations?"

Trauma is not something preached, but it is something shared. It is one beggar telling another beggar where there's food. It is witnessing God's resurrecting power, his power that unleashed a new life out of your own trauma. It is embracing the potential consequences of transparency and vulnerability as you open your heart and lead others toward God's grace.

Through Jesus, God's own heart is given, crushed, and lifted up so that the whole world may be healed. Did Jesus fear the consequences of our salvation? Well, Jesus sweat blood in the Garden. Did he know at that time, the consequences of saving us when he went to war for us? Did he take on every evil, every sin, and every trauma so that we might have life, and have it abundantly, and do it without pain, suffering, and fear? I think he did, because God wanted His Son to know human suffering, pain, and fear, so that we would be out of excuses to deny God and God's love for us. Now, were we worth the cost? We could never afford the price Jesus paid. In fact, we deserve nothing. But in Christ, God has given us everything. And continues to heal us and save us in spite of our inability to the cover the cost. This is all Good News of Great Joy!

Reader's Theatre

Act 3, Scene 6: The Final Blessing

All the attendees are now seated in the sanctuary. The speaker walks to the pulpit and begins.

SPEAKER: To begin the final leg of our journey, I've chosen a story about Moses taken from Numbers 21. It reads like this:

> "...and the Israelites spoke out against God and Moses, "Why have you brought us up out of Egypt to die in the wilderness?" Then the Lord sent poisonous snakes...and they bit the people and many died. The people then came to Moses and said, 'We have sinned. Pray to the Lord to take away the serpents.' ... and the Lord said to Moses, "Make a fiery serpent, and set it on a pole, and everyone who is bitten, shall look at it, and live."

> Now how many of you have ever preached on Moses and the snakes? (*Only three people raise their hands.*) Not many. How come?

LUCY: It's creepy.
SPEAKER: How is it creepy?

LUCY: It's "snakes on a plane" creepy. These people were just bitten by snakes, and then God tells Moses to use what just bit them… (*She pauses, realization dawning.*)…to use what just bit them, what just traumatized them, as the way to heal them!

SPEAKER (*pausing*): Hm-m-m-m. But that's not what the people wanted.

LUCY: No. They wanted God to (*another realization dawning*)…to take away the snakes.

SPEAKER: So what did they want God to do with their snakes?

LUCY: They wanted them gone—out of sight, out of mind, gone! (*Another realization dawns.*) Oh my! They wanted the trauma buried—buried and forgotten! (*The audience reacts with "Wow-ow-ow!"*)

SPEAKER: So! They asked God to help them to make the snakes disappear, to bury them and forget them. If God had done that, what do you think would've happened *again*?

LUCY (*singing*): I'm Hen-e-ry the Eighth I am…Hen-e-ry the Eighth I am, I… (*The audience laughs.*)

SPEAKER (*laughing, waits for crowd to settle*): We should go into partnership!

LUCY: But only if you become—

SPEAKER (*interrupting*): I know, I know—a Wolverine! (*The audience chuckles.*) So, Moses served them "snake on a stick" so that they could learn something and not do the same thing over and over again. God took their trauma, stuck it in their face, and said, "Look at it. Look at your trauma …and live!"

And just in case we missed the point, the Traumatized One said:

> "*Just as Moses lifted up the serpent in the wilderness, so must the Son of Man be lifted up, that whoever believes in him may have eternal life.*" (*He pauses.*) So what does it mean that God would heal people this way?

MARK: God can redeem any trauma—from snakes on a stick to a dead Son on a bigger stick.

SPEAKER: What does it say? That we don't see God using our own traumas to heal us? How could we miss something so...so obvious?

JOHN: Not a bunch of geniuses, that's for sure! (*The audience chuckles.*)

SPEAKER: No, we're not. So tell me, what other places on this planet has the good news of trauma's redemption been realized? What is the best the world can offer the traumatized? Think about it. What is the best thing the world can give to people who are suffering?

JOHN: That which doesn't kill me makes me stronger?

SPEAKER: That which does not kill me makes me stronger. That's it? That's all there is? That's the good news? Is there no hope, no love, no care, and no God?

MARK: We need to *live* the good news to show that there is good news!

SPEAKER: And that good news is...is what?

MARK: The good news is God has redeemed my snakes and has used them...to heal me.

LUCY: Pick up your snakes and follow Me! (*The audience laughs.*)

SPEAKER (*waiting*): Got plenty of those wiggling around. Now I'm shifting gears a little, but the next thing you can do is take a look at the stained-glass windows all around you. Take a good look! Now what do you see?

AUDIENCE: Beautiful ...colorful ...wonderful ...gorgeous!

SPEAKER: Yes, they are all that and more. There are plenty of windows, so get up and get close to the nearest one. (*He waits for the audience to move closer to the windows.*) Now tell each other, what do you see *now*?

MARK (*pausing*): It's not as gorgeous.

LUCY: The colors are still there, but they're not as noticeable...for some reason.

JOHN: Soldering.

MARK AND LUCY: What?

JOHN: Soldering. I see what's soldered, the stuff that holds the glass in place. Didn't notice it far away, but now, right next to it, it's...it's—

MARK AND LUCY (*interrupting*): It's *obvious!*

JOHN: The soldering lines that are throughout the stained-glass windows...

LUCY: Kinda ruin the effect of the stained glass.

MARK: Well, yeah, this close it does. But not from afar.

LUCY: It's still the same beautiful window, but standing here closer to it, it's just different.

SPEAKER: Please return to your seats. (*He pauses.*) From what I heard, most of you concluded that the soldering, the stuff holding the glass pieces together, became visible when you got close. Is that accurate?

AUDIENCE: Yes.

SPEAKER: And yet, from where you are now sitting, is it still beautiful?

AUDIENCE: Yes.

SPEAKER: So the closer you get to a beautiful stained-glass window, the clearer the soldering lines become, right?

AUDIENCE: Yes.

SPEAKER: Those beautiful stained-glass windows, they represent our personalities. When God's light shines through our personalities, we, like those windows, are beautiful, unique, and colorful.

The soldering lines holding the glass in place are the lines of trauma we have experienced in life. Those trauma lines—like soldering lines—are unseen, enveloped by the beauty of personality, but only from a distance. The closer you get to another human being, the more you can see their trauma lines.

JOHN: The unique pattern of the soldering, the trauma lines, makes the windows gorgeous. (*Realization dawns on him.*) Is it God's handiwork to take our traumas and make us...beautiful?

SPEAKER: God is the ultimate potter, taking all of us, cracked pots, and remaking us anew, beautiful, and useful, useful for God's own purpose.

JOHN: But for what's purpose?

MARK: To get close enough to others and see the trauma lines?

SPEAKER: Yes, that's part of it. But there's more.

LUCY: Is the ministry getting close and being respectful of the trauma lines?

SPEAKER: Yes, and still more.

JOHN: Is it holding both their beauty *and* their trauma in your heart?

SPEAKER: Yes! Now that is artistry—God's handiwork. We get close enough to see them, respect them, and then hold them in our hearts, just like how God holds our beauty and trauma in His own heart. (*He pauses.*)

LUCY (*whispering*): Your sign! Your dream! The angel put the sign *in your heart!*

JOHN (*becoming tearful*): Holding us...all...in God's heart

MARK: So we can hold others in ours.

SPEAKER: And then we hold them up to the heart of all the hearts, the one whose very heart became traumatized for us. (*The audience responds with amens.*)

MARK (*pausing*): And that's it?

SPEAKER: Is there any greater challenge than to give you heartaway for another human being, in the same way that God's own heart was given to us?

MARK: No, not really. It's just...just so—

LUCY (*interrupting*): So obvious! (*The audience laughs.*)

JOHN: Even a genius could figure it out!

SPEAKER: So go home! Go home with what brought you to this place. Go home with God's grace, God's courage, and Godspeed. Thank you for sharing this time together. Thank you for bringing your hearts up. And now, go—with your hearts full and in peace. Serve the Lord!

AUDIENCE: Thanks be to God!

Discussion Questions

1. What do you make of the "bury the snakes" request of God to remove the trauma? What do you think of God's creative solution to heal, to go directly at the trauma rather than just removing the snakes? Is the trauma what the people

wanted to be reminded of? Is it a pleasant thing for people in the Passover Meal to be reminded of their trauma of being slaves? How come God doesn't just remove trauma, but rather, God takes and transforms it? Does the Passover remind us of a trauma transformed into a blessing? Is not Hanukah also a trauma transformed blessing? How about the cross?

2.   How does knowing we are all stained glass help you see both the beauty and the traumas in yourself and others? The closer you get to others, the more you see their trauma lines. Similarly, the closer you are with another person, the easier it is for them to see your lines too. Therefore, what are its implications in the way we approach each other? How important is reconciliation? Forgiveness? And mercy?

Possible Responses to DQ

1.   Facing your trauma and its causes is the first step of heal-ing. It allows you not just to face your fear, anger, or embar-rassment, but to accept them as well. If wounds from the traumatic experiences continue to hurt and burn, then the trauma has not healed yet. There may be more trauma bur-ied underneath the trauma that is visible. This is why trans-formation is the key, because instead of burying or remov-ing, embracing the trauma and growing from and with it is what God intended. This is why the act of the Passion of Christ serves as the greatest sign of love; Jesus bore all our wounds and our trauma. He experienced it alone, and faced it so greatly for it to be the symbol of unconditional love and forgiveness. A sign for us to grow, improve, and move forward.

2.   Knowing that we are all stained glass teaches us how to properly approach the people around us. It allows us to be appreciative of one's beauty from afar—their personality, attitude, and other external features and behaviors. At the

same time, the stained-glass analogy teaches us how to be observant and careful with others. It shows us the no one is perfect no matter how beautiful or perfect they may seem. Everyone of us have had a trauma, and with the knowledge that trauma can be healed, we should encourage other people to the God who specializes in healing us.

APPENDIX 1:

Trauma Theory, Theology, and the Three Goals

Goal 1: The Trauma Translation

The first step towards trauma healing is to translate trauma into a language. A language framework is absolutely crucial in making meaningful sense of trauma experiences.

Therefore, in order to provide a trauma-language framework, we need to begin with the building blocks of language, namely, words.

Words have a powerful effect on the brain because they function as brain activators. When meaningfully strung together, words provide a framework to make sense out of life experiences, to converse with one another, and to understand the world around us. Consequently, the framework that enables the brain to process organize, and store life experience for future decision-making is partially a function of language.

With language, the brain is like a wood chipper. Wood chippers take appropriately sized branches, turn them into mulch that is stored in the barn to support future life and growth. Similarly, our brain is also busy mulching life events and then storing them in our memory barn for future decision making. This mulch, when used to support life and growth, is called "learning." Consequently, when we use such learning to make decisions that are for the best interest of ourselves and the people around us, we transform the raw learnings into wisdom. As you may recall, the Bible summarizes this wisdom with the words: "Love your neighbor as yourself."

However, when the logs are too large to process, the wood chipper gets jammed. Similarly, the "brain chipper" also gets jammed with life events that are simply too large to process—or basically, the trauma. When trauma events jam us up, we feel overwhelmed and threatened, making us feel powerless, vulnerable, out of control, and in mortal danger.

The good news is that brain can be unjammed within a short time. Taking the shortcut, it is unjammed by throwing the trauma logs out of the processor and into memory storage. However, though they can be stored there, the logs are in fact stored un-mulched. These un-mulched trauma events are stored in isolation, separate from processed, mulched memory. Doing such shortcut frees up the processor for ongoing life experiences. However, it gives people the false impression that all is already well, the danger has been gone, and it is time to finally move on.

But in reality, all is not well. The problem is that the brain cannot distinguish between the present danger and the stored, unprocessed trauma. To the brain, and when triggered, it can re-run the trauma from the past as if it is still happening in the present. Then, the lower part of the brain sends out the danger signal, and we automatically go into the survival reactions of fight, flight, or freeze. These reactions, when triggered from post-trauma memory, are called "post-trauma reactions."

These post-trauma reactions triggered by un-mulched trauma events are disconnected from our awareness. Unlike processed memory which can be accessed as learning by the creative and logical parts of the brain, there is no learning from unprocessed memory. It's simply forgotten, buried under the mythology that all is well, and it is time to move on. Even when post-trauma reactions come without warning— the odd, embarrassing or even potentially dangerous reactions—the dots between the reactions and the trauma never seem to get connected.

These unpredictable reactions are triggered when current experience accidentally becomes connected or related to the stored energy of the raw and unprocessed trauma memory of the past. Like an electrical discharge of stored energy, even a tangential connection to the trauma memory can surprisingly shock others with confusion, leaving them to wonder, "What was that all about? Why did they react that way to what was done [said, felt]?" Children's questions seem to get to the heart of post-trauma reaction: "Why are they so mean [so cranky, so grumpy]?" or "Why don't they see us anymore [talk to us, go with us, come to church]?"

Because of post-trauma reaction, a person could become a mystery to others. They need to be solved before they can be understood. In a worse scenario, a traumatized person could become alienated from others, saddled with diagnoses like, "They are just not themselves" or "That's just their personality." Without trauma language to provide the framework, to process and integrate trauma into learning, people will continue using the post-trauma survival reactions of fight, flight, or freeze. They will use such reactions to solve the current triggering problems, leaving themselves open to being labeled as odd, strange, weird, unpredictable, and others.

Using non-rational trauma-survival skills to solve current problems of living is not helpful neither. In fact, it even creates a new set of problems to be solved. The new problems could come in forms of making issues more complicated, being disconnected form others, or increased self-isolation. Sometimes, these reactions can result in potentially life-threatening or even evil consequences, thereby traumatizing others as well.

The good news is that through a trauma-language framework, the brain's processor can reboot and start to process, understand, and integrate trauma events once again. Trauma language also empowers the traumatized to meaningfully describe, recognize, and process trauma symptoms and post trauma reactions. Without a common language, traumatic experiences cannot be shared, normalized, or used creatively or logically. The ability to use language and share our trauma unites us as human beings and unleashes trauma's encased energy.

In summary, trauma language, therefore, is the key for living with and through trauma. But without a language to frame, share, or process the trauma events, the unprocessed events are dumped into isolated memory in the backyard of the mind. The backyard dump sites are then covered by rationalizations like,

"I'm done with that"

"It happened so long ago."

"I just forgot about it."

"I just decided to move on."

"As long as we don't bring it up, it can't hurt us."

"There is nothing wrong with moving on!"

The popular myth is that using these rationalizations "helps me deal with it". Unfortunately, these rationalizations do not process or deal with trauma at all. Instead, it cut off our awareness of the presence of ourtraumatic memories. However, despite our unawareness, trauma memory still exerts its energy whenever spontaneously triggered. Accumulated, buried, unprocessed trauma can be called a mental toxic waste site. It eventually poisons the deep rivers of human empathy, limiting human capability and compromising the foundation of our spirituality. Exposure to sights, sounds, words, images, or actions that are even tangentially connected to the trauma events can trigger post-trauma reactions. These odd, strange, inappropriate reactions are the footprints of the forgotten that trauma memories in our backyard.

Therefore, unprocessed trauma, like any toxic waste, needs to be processed and recycled. It need not be buried. With trauma language, the backyard burials stop, and the old sites are excavated, recycled, and redeemed. The first goal, therefore, is to provide a trauma language to establish common ground for healing post-trauma conversations.

Goal 2: The Post Trauma Conversation

With a common trauma language, the post trauma conversation begins.

Ironically, the church's first post-trauma conversation should have started centuries ago. It should have begun with ancient Rome's adoption of the trauma's symbol, namely the cross. However, the symbol was adopted but the trauma conversation was left out.

Leaving out the conversation resulted in a huge piece of biting irony. Even though congregations continued to gather underneath the symbol and profess faith in the One who was traumatized on it, only few could articulate the good news that God enters all trauma conversation and redeems, raises, and empowers all for the same mission.

The mission has always been to follow the Traumatized One into the world's trauma conversations. Doing so is an evidence of the God's grace, the God who redeems, resurrects, and heals trauma. God exists, and the evidence of that healing presence is observed through post-trauma growth.

However, without intentional trauma conversations and the structures to support and encourage them, church trauma accumulates the same way as individual trauma—in backyard dump sites. What differentiates individual backyard trauma and collective church-trauma burials is the greater number of shovels needed to bury the collective trauma! The rationalizations to cover the dump sites remain the same, but with one notable addition.

That notable addition is that doctrine, Scripture, or institutional concerns are used to justify the rationalizations for burying the trauma. Rather than following the Traumatized One into the conversation, we avoid it and justify our avoidance with "It's God's will that we just move on", or "Jesus said, 'Forgive your enemies'", or "Love your neighbor". All these and more have been used not to deal with issues, but to bury them instead.

Pulling out Scripture, doctrine, or "for the sake of the greater good" (the church, the budget, the community, etc.) to stop the conversation only renders the church unsafe, unhealthy, and unfaithful. It makes the church unsafe and unhealthy for real spirituality. It makes it unfaithful in following the mission given by the Traumatized One. Without the conversation to debrief, process, and redeem, buried trauma cripples all meaningful conversations of evangelism, stewardship, mission, and outreach.

Therefore, backyard trauma burials do not work neither for individuals nor groups. Our accumulated mental toxic waste poisons our converging deep rivers of human empathy. It limits corporate human-response capability, and reduces our spirituality to mere platitudes that cannot possibly give sanctuary, hospitality, or entrance to the world's traumatized. Without the conversation, the church is unproductive, unsafe, and unhealthy.

The church was created from trauma and baptized into trauma. The reason for its existence is to offer the hope of redemption and growth to a traumatized world. The conversation, therefore, is integral to the church. The church is the keeper of the good news, the good news that there is a God who enters our trauma and redeems it so that we, too, might become empowered to enter it, learn from it, and share our experience, strength, and hope with others. However, without the conversation, good news is never spoken or demonstrated, and tragically, the traumatized are never raised. Instead of resurrection and growth, people are condemned to a lifetime of blind post-trauma reaction.

Thus, the second goal is to empower churches to begin the conversation and support its continuance through organizational structure. The function of the church is to keep the main thing, the core responsibility of the church. This is to be a faithful follower of the Traumatized One and keep the conversations going!

Goal 3: The Trauma Drama

The third goal is to make this book education ready by using a theater format. With only one performance, entire congregations are exposed to trauma language, discovery, and growth through the characters' trauma journey.

This format offers an alternative to the slow, trickle-down educational process of reading a book with only a few participants involved. Connecting to the characters as they make their way toward healing and growth gives people not only the language, but also the hope they need to make the journey from trauma blindness, to trauma understanding and growth, and finally, to trauma empowerment. The good news is that wherever and whenever a trauma is redeemed, it is transformed from being an enemy to becoming our teacher.

APPENDIX 2:

Hopework For Congregational Healing

A Workshop Series Presented by Pastor Ronald
H Wean, M.Div., M.Ed., LPCC

SESSION 1: DEBRIEFING

PART I: INTRODUCTION TO A
TRAUMA HEALING PROTOCOL

TRAUMA HAPPENS

Trauma exposure may happen suddenly, unexpectedly, or accidentally. It may also occur with a deadly force. It may start through expected or unforeseen death due to health deterioration. It may begin with a failed leadership, at home, church, community, or government. The failure to "do the right thing" is called "**Betrayal Trauma**" or "**Leadership Betrayal**".

Leadership Betrayal comes in many forms. It can be, but not limited to:

- verbal and/or physical abuse
- bullying and harassment

- sexual or financial boundary violations
- theft in office
- criminal activities against both adults and children

Abuse, bullying, harassment, boundary, and criminal violations have a particularly onerous impact in faith communities. When God's Shepherds betray, fleece, or abuse God's sheep, the holy space of God's sanctuary stops being safe. Instead, it becomes chaotic, filled with distrust, suspicion, and distancing. In a post-trauma community, transparency disappears, making the community a breeding ground for hidden agendas.

Consequently, God's mission and witness are usurped by the survival strategies of fight, flight, or freeze. Belief and trust in God and in one another become a thing of the past. Faith becomes a casualty of warring factions vying for control. Once again, the Corinthian Church Crises arise.

And yet, faith communities often **resist identifying Leadership Betrayal**. This resistance also negatively impacts the mission, outreach, and community witness to God. Not seeing is also justified by **false cognitive constructs,** such as, "Bad things do not happen here, because we are nice people protected by God." Therefore, with justification not to see or assess the leadership, faith communities continue to enable the abuse, bullying, or criminal activities unabated.

This resistance to diagnosing leadership betrayal is also reinforced with **rationalizations**. Those rationalizations may include:

"They wear the mantle of God,"
"They've been ordained,"
"But they are the Chosen of God,"
"They do so much good,"
"Because I never saw it, it didn't happen."

These rationalizations do not just excuse or minimize what still may be happening, but they also provide a rationalization NOT to ask for help, even after the immediate crisis of leadership has been removed. Rationalizations enable many to say, "We don't need to ask for help from the outside because nothing happened here." or "The problem is gone. End of story."

Most importantly, these rationalizations damage the mission, outreach, and the community witness of God. The larger community's scorn of these rationalizations is well-earned and summarized in 3 words: "Physician, Heal Thyself!" The larger community sees credibility in healthy faith communities proclaiming God's healing by word and by example. An unhealthy, post-traumatic faith community caught up in survival strategies, in denial, and in their unwillingness to address lingering internal problems has little larger-community credibility.

With the removal of the offender, the natural temptation is to "bury" or "cover up" the community's wounds with expedient, dismissive solutions. Often these expedient "Caiphas Solutions" ("It is better that one man die than the whole nation perish") to resolve community problems are ways to mask the symptoms, but not heal the wound. Thus, the new trauma—uninformed—will utter the first and the last benedictory words to the wounded community, "Nothing to see. Just move on. Pray for peace." These words will never replace the true Word of Healing, the Alpha and the Omega.

However, nothing good ever comes from burying a wound. With burial and cover up, the resulting infection becomes unpredictable, expansive, and chronic; and so the negative impact of the trauma continues. Therefore, faith communities need to implement a healing protocol to receive the first gift, the gift of healing. This gift of healing precedes the coming of the other gifts to the community—the gifts of mission, focus, and purpose. Anything less than transformational healing is a preamble to a funeral—the funeral of the faith community.

It's no easy task to heal a faith community with a history of leadership betrayal. Those faith communities who begin to face leadership abuse, bullying, or criminal activities, quickly come to two conclusions:

First: The whole community is wounded.

Second: The wounding is too big for the community to heal by itself.

Just like traumatized individuals, a community cannot think or talk itself out of trauma's impact. The old adage, "Doctors who treat themselves have fools for patients" becomes prophetic in faith communities who don't ask for help. Even if we try self-healing from trauma, the best we can do is create a civil war between our **body sensations** and our brain. The result is a mind full of **racing thoughts**, **anxious mind**, or worse, a **committee of 'shoulds'** which the Scripture calls, "a house divided against itself."

Following trauma, this internal 'should' committee begins self-talks with "I should have intervened...because if I did...I could have stopped the trauma in the faith community. But because I did not intervene, I must be bad, weak, stupid, or crazy."

Unfortunately, the **'should' committee** could go on for months and even years, but still, it never ends in healing. All the time, it fails to change what happened, because people do not have the power to rewrite history. Trauma happens despite what we do or don't. The only power the **'should' committee** has is to send those who listen to it into **dissociation** and **despair**, which could last for years.

The behaviors of a dissociated, despairing faith community can be summarized in three words: "**cranky**, **controlling**, and **numb**." These 3 behaviors are the bear prints outside the trash can. If bear prints are found, there can be only one conclusion, that a bear was there! If cranky, controlling, and numb are present in a faith community, there is only one conclusion as well, that trauma was also there! And sadly, it was never healed!

Being "Cranky, Controlling, and Numb" are the direct result of the unreleased trauma energy, now stored in the body. All the trauma energy is tightly bound, trapped within the body of individuals as well as within the whole Body of Christ. Tightly holding onto that trauma energy shuts down the thinking part of the brain. Without the ability to think clearly, we can't think nor ask for outside help. Creative, logical, empathetic, and informed thinking will not occur without releasing the body's trauma energy first.

Without creativity, logic, empathy, and informed thinking, our ability to problem-solve as individuals and as a community is severely compromised. Without help and a healing protocol, a **post-trau-**

matic church is a thoughtless faith community **STUCK** in being "cranky, controlling, and numb". If you don't believe that a post-traumatic church can be stuck in a "cranky, controlling, and numb" series of reactions, then TRY CHANGING SOMETHING! The bear will surely come out and play with the trash can!

To summarize, the body energy created by trauma exposure needs to be **released, not opposed**. That energy is encoded in the body through body sensations. These body sensations cause the body to tighten, which shuts down the very part of the brain needed for receiving the gift of healing. A tight body is holding onto the trauma energy, producing body sensations, anxious feelings, tension, and racing thoughts,. Ultimately, these make a thoughtful reflection impossible; thus, leaving the person "stuck" in there.

In a relaxed body, the brain is free to engage in "whole brain thinking" of creativity, logic, empathy, and recall. The same is true within a relaxed faith community. In a relaxed community, the ability to think, pair and articulate the body sensations with emotions is present. It allows the church to pause and make sense of what happened, a very crucial aspect of healing. In other words, the relaxed Body of the Faith Community becomes MINDFUL of the impact of the trauma. It is empowered **to receive** the gift of **transformation** from a **surviving to a thriving** faith community.

In the relaxed Body of the Faith Community, **the trauma that tyrannizes** us is transformed into a **teacher that teaches** us to be a **blessing** for a wounded world. Just like how God transformed the crucifixion from trauma into a blessing for the world, God transforms our **pain into purpose** and gives us **hope** and a new name, "**Wounded Healer**". Working together within the "manger" or "incubator" called "a healing protocol," God transforms wounds into blessings for the world. Consequently, trauma transformationis an evidence to the world that God heals and invitesall the wounded to receive His blessings to give to give back to others as well.

HOPEWORK HAPPENS

"HOPEWORK" is what we are called to do as Christians. It is the natural outgrowth of **Bible Study**, **Listening Prayer**, **Mindful Awareness**, **Worship**, **Service**, and **Fellowship.** It takes all of these to empower a community to "Come now and let us reason together" (Isaiah 1:18)—and when we "reason together," we are empowered to develop healthy protocols, incubators, and mangers

Through it, we put ourselves and others in positions to receive God's Gift of healing. As one physician summarized the healing arts, "I show up, do the right thing, and treat people by putting them in positions to receive the gift of healing. Then, I get out of God's Way!"

The doctor never took credit for healing, but always gave credit to God. The recognition that healing is a gift from God gives us a special kind of hope unknown to the world, but is never misplaced. Our hope is always in the God who loves "to heal the sick, raise the dead, and set the captives free."

So, our hope is grounded in God's next act. If the HOPEWORK involves **grief, we work together with hope** and "**reason together**" in forming **grief healing protocols**, because we "do not grieve like the rest of mankind, who have no hope" (I Thessalonians 4:13-18).

In addition to experiencing hope in grief, we are also called to **work together with hope,** and "**reason together**" in forming **wounded faith community protocols**. The Greek word for "trauma," translated, is "wound." Wounded faith communities deal with both **Grief** and **Trauma,** because there is **grief in trauma** and **trauma in grief.** They are just **two different sides** of the **same coin** and need healing protocols to treat both sides.

It is not by accident that grief and trauma are connected. Isaiah 53:4-5 clearly makes this connection, stating, "Surely, he has borne our griefs and carried our sorrows, and by his stripes, his wounds, we are healed and made whole." Consequently, in order for a traumatized church to be in a position to receive the gift of God's healing, faith communities need spiritual, wholistic healing protocols to address both the trauma and the grief of the community.

The need for spiritual, wholistic healing protocols was illustrated by a secular study of post-traumatic police officers. Professor Chopka of Kent State University stated, "The best predictor of post-trauma growth is spirituality." (Ohio Counselors Association Assembly, Columbus, Ohio, 2013). The results of that study might have surprised some counselors, but not faith communities who recognize that healing is a gift from the God who loves to heal the broken by transforming our wounds into blessings for the world.

Healing from trauma in churches is **not** usually quick. It does not arrive from an expedient fix of **symptom control.** People cannot be shamed into burying the energy of the hurt and pain of being betrayed by church leadership. Trying to fix the community's pain by making them feel inadequate and by telling them, "you need to pray more" or "get more faith" or "get over it" or "go somewhere else", is an invitation to a funeral, not a celebration of community healing. However, without the container of a healing protocol, shaming becomes the default protocol, despite proving that it never works, over and over again. Holding onto the expectation that this time, the outcome will be different, is not a sign of a positive mental health.

Praying is a crucial part in the healing of any disease. We are commanded to "pray for the sick." But praying does not mean we address wounds without a healing protocol. **Prayer and Protocol** sets the stage for God to do God's finest work—to heal the core of the wound, not just the edges.

The 5 Tasks of the healing protocol are: **Debriefing, Processing, Integrating, Transforming, and Planning.**

Part 1: THE FIRST TASK OF THE HEALING PROTOCOL—DEBRIEFING

The first of the five stages in addressing the wound is Debriefing. Debriefing requires a safe environment where **identifying** the wound is made possible. A safe environment begins when God is invited. When God is invited, we are assured that God **shows up every time**, because, "…where 2 or 3 are gathered together in my name, there am I in their midst" (Matthew 18:20).

A **safe environment** occurs when the leadership **prays** for **God's presence, acknowledges** the **wound**, and **normalizes** the **feelings, thoughts,** and **reactions** arising from the wound. Leadership **validates** the congregation's **strength and courage** to **survive**, or to **keep coming back**. It validates their **attempts to heal**, or their willingness **to share** their **pain**. The safe environment is established when that same process of praying, acknowledging, normalizing, and validating has **already begun** with the leadership.

A **safe environment**, therefore, happens **without judgment** or **attempts to fix others**, their **pain**, or their **situations**. Only God is qualified to judge or fix. We just need to get out of God's Way!

A **safe environment** needs to be **confidential**. Whatever is said in the meeting, what is heard in the meeting, stays in the meeting.

QUESTION #1: HOW HAVE YOU MADE THE **ENVIRONMENT SAFE FOR YOUR CONGREGATION TO HEAL?**

DEBRIEFING LAYS THE **GROUNDWORK FOR HOPE** THROUGH **UNDERSTANDING OUR "WIRING."** "Our Wiring" **begins with the Body** because, "Your Body is the Temple of the Holy Spirit" (I Cor. 6:19-20). God begins with the body in creation, **breathes the breath** or wind of God into a clod of earth, and a living being is created and **begins to move.** (Genesis 2:7-8). When grieving or wounded, it "takes my breath away" or "I felt like my life was being squeezed out of me" or "It took my legs right out from under me". Therefore, healing begins when the body relearns **how to breath, how to relax tightened muscles,** and **how to move.**

QUESTION #2: WHEN GRIEVING OR WOUNDED, WHAT ARE THE FIRST 2 PROCESSES THAT SHUT OFF?

The Body controls how you think, feel, and move. We don't have a body; we are our bodies. The Body does 4 things: The Body always **TELLS THE TRUTH, REMEMBERS EVERYTHING, KEEPS THE SCORE,** and **GOES ON STRIKE (stops breathing and moving, breaks down, becomes ill) WHEN WE DO NOT LISTEN TO IT.** Therefore, practicing intentional "consistent deep belly baby breathing", pelvic relaxation, and intentional body movement" is required.

BODY LISTENING EXERCISES

EXERCISE #1: Baby belly breathing: Place your hands on your chest. Now, breathe without moving your chest. Breathe in through the nose on the 5 count, hold it for 2 counts, and then completely exhale through your mouth on the 6 count. How does your body feel?

EXERCISE #2: Squeeze your pelvic region as hard as you can for 10 seconds. Now, let your belly just flop/relax and take 2 SLOW deep baby breaths in through the nose, out through the mouth.

EXERCISE #3: Sit quietly in a chair for one minute. After one minute, where do you feel the most pressure?

QUESTION #3: WHAT DO YOU EXPERIENCE AFTER RELAXING THE PELVIC FLOOR AND THE SLOW BREATHS?

QUESTION #4: WHAT DOES THIS TELL YOU ABOUT WHAT YOUR BODY NEEDS IN ORDER TO MANAGE YOUR STRESS?

QUESTION #5: HOW WOULD THIS EXERCISE HELP PEOPLE IN DEBRIEFING THEIR WOUNDS? QUESTION #6: HOW WOULD YOU MODEL THIS IN HELPING PEOPLE HEAL?

EXERCISE #4: MAKING CONNECTIONS WITH OTHERS.

On a neurological level, we are wired for community living. We are neurologically wired for **JOY** (dopamine), **PEACE** (serotonin), and **CONNECTION** (endorphins). In a healthy, prenatal and birth environment, the wiring begins in the womb and continues through life. Through neuro-plasticity, we are able to learn, use logic, reason, and recall - in other words, with this "hard wiring," we can add software to our brains! From this balance, we learn how to think **creatively, logically, and empathetically, within an accumulated knowledge pool and training**. When **activated**, we can act in our own and others' best interests within a community using wisdom and understanding.

The gifts of this system are:

- **increasing awareness of Self-God-Others**;
- **decreasing sense of self-seriousness**—coupled with an:
- increasing ability to recognize and laugh at ourselves.

We are also given the gifts of exploring **adventures and partnering with God and one another**:

- **to fully engage in mission** equipped with all that we need for ministry,
- **to negotiate mission direction** with others,
- **to discover a vision** of where God wants you to be in God's plan of healing the world, and
- **to faithfully follow through** with **joy** while living in a dark world.

This is our witness to the power of God's presence.

If, however, the child has been raised in an unhealthy environment with fear, anger, loss, wounding, violence, stress, or betrayal, on a neurological level, the designed gifts of God's wiring do not usually happen. The brain becomes wired on adrenaline and cortisol with the survival skills of hyper-vigilance—fight, flight, or freeze.

QUESTION #7: WHAT ARE THE HEALTH RISKS OF LONG-TERM EXPOSURE TO ADRENALINE AND CORTISOL?

QUESTION #8: WHAT IS THE PRIMARY FEELING OF PEOPLE WITH LONG TERM EXPOSURE TO ADRENALINE AND CORTISOL AND HOW DO THEY REACT TO THE WORLD? TO TRIGGERS?

QUESTION #9: WHAT ARE THE EFFECTS ON THE BODY OF CHRIST TO HAVE FEAR-BASED DECISION-MAKING?

HOPEWORK HOMEWORK #1

Before the next meeting, **PLEASE:**

1. PRACTICE BREATHING, PELVIC RELAXATION, AND BODY MOVEMENT.
2. WRITE OUT YOUR TIMELINE OF LOSS AND WOUNDING FROM CHILDHOOD TO NOW.
3. CHOOSE AT LEAST ONE LOSS OR WOUNDING AND ANSWER THE FOLLOWING QUESTIONS:

   What happened? What was my experience of it? What was the worst thing I experienced in the event? What body sensations did I feel? Who helped me through the event? What did they say or do that was helpful? How did the event change me? When I think of it now, what sensations, feelings, thoughts, and reactions do I have? Have I talked with God about what happened? As a result of all that happened, what am I like now?

SESSION 2: DEBRIEFING EXERCISES

INTRODUCTION: 4 Parts to a Congregational
Trauma Healing Protocol

DEBRIEFING: A debriefing process assists the wounded in recovering their **breath, mind, body**, and their **choice**. The goal of a debriefing is to stimulates **thinking rather than reacting** to the wounds within an empowered group. An empowered group is made up of people who **"get it,"** and who are also **understanding** and **knowledgeable** about self-wound care, and who **can LISTEN**.

PROCESSING: Group processing is the most effective intervention for wound care. The goal of Processing is to **make meaning** out of the wounds by asking the questions, "What do these wounds in my body / my thoughts **tell me** about myself, God, and the world?" And "What is God asking me to do with these wounds?"

INTEGRATING INTO MY/OUR STORY: The story is not about how I **didn't survive** my wounds, but how God has led me to **thrive and triumph through**, **despite**, and **because** of them. This is **the legacy of your witness** to the God who heals.

TRANSFORMATION: The **willingness to listen** and then appropriately **share** how God has breathed **new life, direction, and purpose** into my life through **pain and suffering**.

STEP 1: **CREATING SAFETY**
- **Create safety in self** through **prayer listening, breathing listening**, and **body listening** (relaxation of the pelvic floor and "mindfulness,").
    - If your **brain goes off-line,** you will react with **fight, flight, freeze**, or **pain fixing** attempts using disputation, argument, or even the misuse of Scripture.
    - When your brain goes off-line, you will not be able to think or respond **creatively, logically, empathetically**, or **employ recall** to access **previous experience**, knowledge, understanding, or **wisdom**.

- The "off-line brain is unable to **breathe, move, or listen** even to self or God, and may go into **self-shaming** ("what's the matter with me?") or fear ("I can't do this!"). These results in **dissociation** ("just bury it and forget about it!")

- Therefore, you need **to practice "deep belly baby breathing"**, **listening prayer**, and **body listening** as preparation to receive God's gift of self-understanding. Your gift is being invited to partner with God, in His Adventure, His Mission to heal the wounded by receiving the **healing God wants you** to have for your wounds.

LISTENING PRAYER FOR PREPARATION: Waiting for God to speak back

"Silence is the language of God who expects us to become fluent in that language."

Presider: Thank You, God, for all the gifts You have given us: our minds, our bodies, our abilities to think, move, and breathe. Thank you for all the tough times, the harsh times, when you put us on a solid rock and saved us. We praise you, God, for breathing into us when our own breath was taken away.

PEOPLE: Breathe into us again, O God. Give us the breath that lifts our hearts, orders our thoughts, silences the noise, calms our fears, increases our faith, and allows us to think. Help us listen, lean into the silence, and learn from the "still small voice" calling us as You transform our pain into blessings for others. In Jesus' name, we wait for Your Breath.

BREATHE INTO OUR SILENCE: WE ARE LISTENING
(pause, listen)

Presider: Thank You, God, for Your transforming silence, a place where pain is transformed into wisdom, suffering into self-understanding, and where wounds are changed into witnesses of Your Healing—a healing that gives us life, and gives it abundantly.

PEOPLE: Breathe into us again, O God! Help us to witness Your transforming power. Use our wounds to proclaim Your healing presence. As You raised the cross from a curse to a Blessing, raise us to be blessings for others. In Jesus' name, we wait for Your breath.

BREATHE INTO OUR SILENCE: WE ARE LISTENING
(pause, listen)

Presider: We have done nothing to deserve Your call to be Your partners. Thank You for forgiving us, healing us, and inviting us, as co-workers with You. Use our wounds, as You used the wounds of Christ, to breathe healing and life to the wounded.

PEOPLE: Breathe into us, O God, a voice of compassion for the wounded, grace for the grieving, and mercy for the suffering. Give us breath to speak with tenderness and wisdom, born from our own suffering and healing. Make us into Your Wounded Healers. In Jesus' name, we wait for Your Breath.

BREATHE INTO OUR SILENCE: WE ARE LISTENING
(pause, listen)

Presider: Let no fear paralyze us. Let no worry stop us. Let no anxiety dissuade us from Your focus. Breathe into us, so that we become better tools in Your great plan to heal the world.

PEOPLE: Protect us from the lies of fear. Breathe into us Your Spirit of Truth, that You have already equipped us so that we can do all things through You.

BREATHE INTO OUR SILENCE: WE ARE LISTENING
(pause, listen)

HOW DO WE CREATE SAFETY IN RELATIONSHIPS?

- **Create safety in relationships** through:

- listening to others **without judgement** or fixing their problem
- **accepting** others **as human beings** who have been **wounded**
- **validating** what they have **been through** and the **wounds they carry**
- **normalizing** their **feelings and survival** reactions
- **lifting up** their **strength and courage** in their **attempts to survive** and to **carry on despite the wound**s
- **Anonymity:** What is said here, remains here; important in building trust
- **Time limits:** Sharing needs to be no more than 5 minutes. Additional time after group can be given.

PRACTICE BEING THE SPEAKER, THE LISTENER, THE OBSERVER

We can choose to be either a speaker, a listener, or an observer in conversations. We can only be one at a time. Making a conscious choice to speak, to listen, or to observe depends on the role you choose. In your group of 3, each of you will have the opportunity to practice all three roles, but not at the same time! As a speaker, you need to speak in a manner that communicates your experience. The listener needs to assure the speaker that the listener is listening, but not with words. The observer needs to observe the interaction of the speaker and listener and how they are communicating.

GROUP ROTATION: The speaker speaks the story. The listener listens to the story without speaking. The observer who observes and notices both interacting from a bigger picture, also does not speak.

ASSIGNMENT FROM TIMELINE: Answer the questions: "What do these **wounds in my body / my thoughts tells me** about myself, God, and the world?" and "**What is God asking me to**

do with these wounds?" "Are there any recurring **themes**? **Motifs**? **Roadblocks**?" "Has anything happened **before**?"

SESSION 3: PROCESSING THE GRIEF IN THE WOUND AND THE WOUND IN THE GRIEF

LISTENING PRAYER FOR PREPARATION: Waiting for God to speak back
"Silence is the language of God who expects us to become fluent in that language."

Presider: Thank You, God, for all the gifts You have given us—our minds, our bodies, our ability to think and move and breathe. Thank you for all the tough times, the harsh times, when you put us on a solid rock and saved us. We praise you, God, for breathing into us when our own breath was taken away.
PEOPLE: Breathe into us again, O God. Give us the breath that lifts our hearts, orders our thoughts, silences the noise, calms our fears, increases our faith, and allows us to think. Help us listen, lean into the silence, and learn from the "still small voice" calling us as You transform our pain into blessings for others. In Jesus' name, we wait for Your Breath.

BREATHE INTO OUR SILENCE: WE ARE LISTENING
(pause, listen)

Presider: Thank You, God, for Your transforming silence, a place where pain is transformed into wisdom, suffering into self-understanding, and where wounds are changed into witnesses of Your Healing, a healing that gives us life, and gives it abundantly.
PEOPLE: Breathe into us again, O God! Help us witness Your transforming power. Use our wounds to proclaim Your healing presence. As You raised the cross from a curse to a Blessing, raise us to be blessings for others. In Jesus' name, we wait for Your breath.

BREATHE INTO OUR SILENCE: WE ARE LISTENING
(pause, listen)

Presider: We have done nothing to deserve Your Call to be Your Partners. Thank You for forgiving us, healing and inviting us, as co-workers with You. Use our wounds, as You used the wounds of Christ, to breathe healing and life to the wounded.

PEOPLE: Breathe into us, O God, a voice of compassion for the wounded, grace for the grieving, and mercy for the suffering. Give us breath to speak with tenderness and wisdom, born from our own suffering and healing. Make us into Your wounded healers. In Jesus' name, we wait for Your breath.

BREATHE INTO OUR SILENCE: WE ARE LISTENING
(pause, listen)

Presider: Let no fear paralyze us. Let no worry stop us. Let no anxiety dissuade us from Your focus. Breathe into us, so that we become better tools in Your Great Plan to Heal the World.

PEOPLE: Protect us from the lies of fear. Breathe into us Your spirit of truth, that You have already equipped us so that we can do all things through You.

BREATHE INTO OUR SILENCE: WE ARE LISTENING
(pause, listen)

PART 1: MOURNING THE LOSS
OF FALSE COGNITIVE 207

CONSTRUCTS OF REALITY.
- We don't want the world to be **a scary place**. (versus the 24 hour news cycle of 9-11), (Coronavirus)
- We want to make the world **a safer place** to experience peace. ("We are the World. We are the Children"—U.S.A. for Africa; "I'd Like to Buy the World a Coke"—Coca-Cola)

- We make **assumptions** about reality based on our **entitlements**—what we want, feel, and need. ("The World Owes Me a Living" – Shirley Temple)
- We make **investments** in life based on those assumptions. (We "bet the farm" that what we assume to be true, is true). Then, we develop a **Vision and Mission** of our lives based on our assumptions that we believe are true.
- When reality is the **opposite** or does not live up to our **life assumptions**, what did you experience? Fear, loss, betrayal, disappointment, anger, sadness, visceral reactions, bitterness, loss of faith, threat...? Who do we blame? God? Others? Ourselves?
- When we experience/perceive our **lives are threatened**, we react by tightening and shallow breathing, turning off our thinking and replacing with **fight-flight-freeze** reactivity, because the **meaning** of our lives **has been shattered**, our **vision of ourselves** is now **gone**, and our mission is **no place** (utopos). "Non Sui, sui, non sui, non Caro (I was not, I am, I am not, I care not)"
- The key is to **hold on to community** despite the pain and bitterness, **identify what was lost**—but with safe people—and **commit** to make the wound **your new teacher in finding a new vision**, and a **new mission** by **connecting** with others who were also wounded.

PART 2: EXERCISE: Exploring constructs we place on the world, God, others, and ourselves.

- Prepare to read the questions by **Relaxing** the Pelvic Floor with 5-2-6 **Deep Belly Baby Breathing. Keep Breathing** throughout the Exercise!
- Take 5 minutes and place a mark besides each **assumption** you thought **was true** about the world, God, people:
  1. God never gives you more than you can bear.
  2. If we just ignore it, it will go away.

3. All pastors, priests, and rabbis are good people and would never hurt us.
4. All teachers, principals, doctors, and counselors are good people and would never hurt us.
5. I thought I would remain married 'til death do us part.
6. I thought I would die before my spouse.
7. I thought I would die before my child.
8. Nothing bad will ever happen to my family, because we are nice people.
9. Nothing bad will ever happen to my church, because we are a nice church.
10. I could avoid tragedy, poverty, sickness, evil people, and death if I do all the right things and say all the right prayers.
11. God is testing us by all the bad things that happened in my church.
12. I thought my church would understand me.
13. I thought everyone in my church loved each other.
14. I thought I lived in a safe neighborhood.
15. I never thought I would pray, "Where are you, God? Why have you abandoned me?"

- Take another 5 minutes and choose one of the marked ones and answer the following questions:
    - When did you realize your life assumption(s) were not true?
    - What reaction(s) did you have?
    - How did this affect your relationship with God? Prayer Life?
    - Who did you talk to and what did they say or do that was helpful?
    - When you look back at it, where was God and what did God do in the midst of your pain?

- Divide into **Groups of Three** with Speaker, Listener, Observer. Take 5 minutes apiece to share your answers and then rotate. Again, relax and breathe from the belly.
- Large Group **Debriefing**

PART 3: REVIEW OF HOPEWORK HOMEWORK

ASSIGNMENT #1

- Review the HOPEWORK ASSIGNMENT: Within your GROUPS OF THREE: SPEAKER-LISTENER-OBSERVER
- Large Group Debriefing

HOPEWORK HOMEWORK ASSIGNMENT #2 in Two Weeks: What is the vision behind my narrative?

- Am I any **different** than I was before my wound(s)?
- In what ways am I more **bitter, jaded**, or **positive through gratitude**?
- What are my **scarred-over wounds** teaching me about myself, others, God, and the world?
- What **Vision** of myself do I have now when I look at my scabbed wounds?
- What **new gifts** do I bring to the Lord's table?
- What **Mission** am I beginning to discern for which God is calling me?
- When I leave and go to be with the Lord, what **legacy of encouragement** do I want to leave behind for those who will follow me?

SESSION FOUR: THE NARRATIVE OF YOUR JOURNEY

HOPEWORK JOURNEY SUMMARIZED

1. DEBRIEFING: Re-Integrating Body-Mind-Spirit after the Journey of Wound and Loss
2. PROCESSING: Make meaning of the journey
3. INTEGRATING INTO A NARRATIVE: A Cohesive Story of Your Journey

LISTENING PRAYER FOR PREPARATION: Waiting for God to speak back

"Silence is the language of God who expects us to become fluent in that language."

Presider: I will not lie down in the desert of wounds. This is not my destiny. I am on a quest.

Though the grasslands have browned, the ground has cracked, and the night is full of the unknown, I sense a presence.

PEOPLE: Breathe into us again, O God. Show us your way to the flood lands of the soul. Raise us up.

Do not let us die in the wilderness, but take us one step and then another toward the waters of renewal and the light of day.

BREATHE INTO OUR SILENCE: WE ARE LISTENING
(pause, listen)

Presider: As I press on into this journey, I will seek out others who understand. We will sit around the campfire and support each other, as we travel together in the deserts of loss and wounds.

People: Breathe Strength into us, O God, to lift up each other for this quest. Breathe trust and confidence into us so that we speak hope, speak purpose, and speak life to each other. Breathe Your Peace into us, so that we know that we are not alone.

BREATHE INTO OUR SILENCE: WE ARE LISTENING
(pause, listen)

215

Presider: Protect me, O God, from the Constrictor of Fear. Give me eyes to see the snake which offers the tempting distraction of relying on myself instead of You.

People: Heavenly Father, breathe courage into us to ask for help from You. Help us to take steps to untangle the coils of the Constrictor from our lives. Help us to focus on You and not on ourselves.

BREATHE INTO OUR SILENCE: WE ARE LISTENING
(pause, listen)

Presider: The Constrictor has done its worst—we are all wounded. We are a pile of rubble in a war torn world. But You, O God, are the Artist.

People: Breathe in us each day, as we continue to clean the rubble of our wounds and turn them over to You. Create beauty and purpose from our pain. Demonstrate to the world Your artistry through us, as You continue to repurpose our rubble into Your best work.

BREATHE INTO OUR SILENCE: WE ARE LISTENING
(pause, listen)

INTRODUCTION: THE RUBBLE OF WAR TORN WARSAW

SMALL GROUPS:
* What did you hear in that story?
* How did it affect you?
* How did they go from surviving to thriving?
* What were their strengths?

THE POWER OF THE NARRATIVE JOURNEY
* Your Story is your history of taking a difficult journey from surviving to thriving

- Your Story imbues confidence in God to take on other "adventures" that life presents
- Your Story illustrates the strengths and gifts that God has given you
- Your Story reinforces the presence of God and God's Power to raise you up
- Your Story replaces the mind clutter, the noise, and the forgetfulness that we survived the journey by the grace of God alone
- Your Story reminds you to live a life of gratitude rather than self-congratulation.

EXAMPLES OF THE POWER OF THE NARRATIVE JOURNEY
- THE SPOKEN JOURNEY: THE SHIP OF GOLD (small group questions above)
- THE SUNG JOURNEY: HYMNS: Horatio Spafford – "It is Well", Tommy Dorsey – "Precious Lord", Henry Lyte –
- "Abide with Me", John Newton – "Amazing Grace", Alexander Means – "What Wondrous Love", Laura Story –
- "Blessings", Robert Keene – "How Firm a Foundation"
- THE WORN JOURNEY: Amish mustaches

QUESTIONS THAT ASSIST YOU IN DISCOVERING YOUR NARRATIVE:
- What happened?
- What did you do?
- What happened next?
- What did you do?
- What was it like?
- How did you make it through?
- Looking back, what was the worst part of the journey?
- What was God doing while you were on this journey? What are you most grateful for?

- Having made it through the journey, how has this experience affected you, the way you view the world, how you live, and your relationships with God and others?

SMALL GROUPS

Using the questions as a guide, take 5 minutes to tell your narrative of one adventure on your timeline.

HOPEWORK ASSIGNMENT #2

1. Identify how you might be blocked in sharing your story with others.
2. Identify how your story might help you listen better to their stories and establish safety.
3. Identify ways to use this training to heal and release others within the congregation.

SESSION FIVE: THE 3 Ps: PAIN, PURPOSE, PLAN

HOPEWORK JOURNEY SUMMARIZED

1. **DEBRIEFING**: The Goal in this step is to **assist the wounded** with the following **wound care: a safe place for the wounded to talk with people who "get it"**, and a safe place by **listening, normalizing** their reactions, **validating** them as people who survived their wounds, and teaching **relaxation and breathing** coping skills to help them **shift** from the **reactor brain** to the **responder brain.**
2. **PROCESSING**: The **Responder** part of the brain has two sides—**Right** and **Left**. The Right side works with the Left side so that the wounded can begin to **make meaning** of their wounds through **Creativity and Empathy** (Right), **Logic and Knowledge** (Left), and **Connection** to an informed, compassionate, and understanding **community**.
3. **INTEGRATING** INTO A NARRATIVE: A cohesive story of Your journey from a wounded **victim**, to a recovering **survivor**, to an empowered **thriver—embracing your**

wounds as your **life teachers** based on the One who **gave us life** through **His Wounds.**

LISTENING PRAYER FOR PREPARATION: Waiting for God to speak back.

"Silence is the language of God who expects us to become fluent in that language."

PRESIDER: We have waited for You in the desert O God. In the heat, we waited for Your word. Parched, we watched for Your next act. We waited and watched for You to fulfill Your promise of living water, but we asked, "Can these dry bones ever live again?"

PEOPLE: WE WAITED FOR THE LIVING WATER TO WELL UP INSIDE US. WE WAITED AND PRAYED THAT YOU WOULD FILL THE WATERS OF OUR SOULS AND SPILL OVER THE BOUNDARIES OF OUR DRY, CRACKED SPIRITS. WE WAITED FOR YOUR SALVATION, O GOD, AND YOU DID NOT DISAPPOINT US. YOU RESCUED US. AS YOU PROMISED, YOU GAVE US YOUR LIVING WATER. THANK YOU FOR GOING INTO OUR DESERT. THANK YOU FOR SEARCHING FOR US. THE LOST ARE NOW FOUND. THE THIRSTY ARE NOW QUENCHED.

BREATHE INTO OUR SILENCE: WE ARE LISTENING
(pause, listen)

PRESIDER: God, You are so good. You fulfilled Your promise and provided us with living water. It wells up inside us and streams throughout all deserts. It rises with volume and heads to pools and watering holes within, around, and through all of our dry and desiccated places.

PEOPLE: MY HEART NOW OVERFLOWS WITH STREAMS OF KINDNESS. IT SURGES FORWARD TO HELP AND REFRESH OTHER DESERT DWELLERS. AND AS I SEARCH AND FIND THE DRY ONES. I WILL SEEK TO SERVE THEM, SO THAT THEY BECOME A SPRING OF NEW LIFE THROUGH ME.

BREATHE INTO OUR SILENCE: WE ARE LISTENING
(pause, listen)

PRESIDER: My heart has changed. I now look forward to life's challenges and God's next Adventure.

PEOPLE: I AM COMMITTED TO THE QUEST OF A RENEWED LIFE. YOU, O GOD, HAVE LEVERAGED MY LOSS INTO LEADING OTHERS TO THE LIVING WATERS. YOU HAVE MADE ME INTO A WARRIOR OF THE SPIRIT, TRAINED TO DEFEND, MENTOR, AND PROTECT THOSE WHO ARE STILL HURT.

BREATHE INTO OUR SILENCE: WE ARE LISTENING
(pause, listen)

THE POWER OF PURPOSE
- Designed for Building Walls or Cathedrals?
- We are designed as "**purpose seeking missiles.**"
- **Purpose is power**: (increases) have more friends, energy, movement, and life satisfaction, rebalances joy, peace, connection, and courage to **tolerate the discomfort zone** of **transformation.** If people have purpose in one area of life, then all areas of their lives will become purpose-driven. A purpose-driven church is a healthy church.
- **The source** of the Power of Purpose comes from **addressing** the pain **from the inside** rather than looking at the pain **from the outside.**
- **Embracing the Pain within** gives people **control—centeredness** inside by **walking through** it, finding ways to live through it, and giving people the **confidence** to continue to solve the problem of Pain from the inside core of who they are. (Recovery Thinking vs. Alcoholic Reasoning)
- **Rage-Blame** indicates that **the pain locus** is external—leaving people feeling powerless because we have little control over people, places, or things (latest gun shooting / lack of limit setting).

220

- Rage-Blame gives only **temporary relief** from the pain, while saddling people into Rage-Blame **survival coping skills** to manage future life problems.
- Examples: Teacher: "I am the key to every door." (powerlessness pain). Orderly: "I keep families together." (special needs pain). Daughter: "What people think doesn't matter because this is who I really am." (rejection pain). "My job is to help you keep yours." (unemployment pain).

EXERCISE #1: What is **Your Purpose**? What is **Your Life Statement**?
- Take 7 minutes by yourselves and write out YOUR PURPOSE FOR LIFE
- Take 10 minutes to share your statement in groups of 3

EXERCISE #2: What is YOUR Purpose to gather in **Church**?
1. Take 7 minutes to clarify and write out your purpose
2. Compare it to your own Life's Purpose Statement
3. Take 10 minutes to share in groups of 3

EXERCISE #3: The New Beginning of the **Church Plan** to Address Pain

- Take 7 minutes and relook at your purpose statements. What is the first thing you feel compelled to do? (It could be to begin a Bible Study, attend Sunday School, have uncomfortable conversations where you need to share your own purpose and how you can help those who are struggling).
- In your groups of 3, share 5 minutes each and answer: what direction
- are you sensing from your purpose statement?
- Get another group of 3 and make a list of their names, what their life statements are, and how they plan to act on it.
- Submit those names, mission statements, and actions to the pastor.

CPSIA information can be obtained
at www.ICGtesting.com
Printed in the USA
JSHW022129060422
24596JS00005B/159